HINDUISM

An Introduction

DHARAM VIR SINGH

Rupa & Co

Concept & Design © Rupa & Co 2003
Copyright © Dharam Vir Singh 2003

Published 2003 by

Rupa & Co

7/16 Ansari Road, Daryaganj
New Delhi 110 002

Sales Centres:
Allahabad, Bangalore, Chandigarh,
Chennai, Dehradun, Hyderabad,
Jaipur, Kaathmandu, Kolkata,
Ludhiana, Mumbai, Pune

Design by
Bagan Sarkar

Cover Photograph
Rajesh Bedi

Typeset by
Capital Creations, Flat No. 4 Subhram Complex
D-96, Munirka, New Delhi - 110 067

Printed in India by
Rekha Printers Pvt. Ltd.
A-102/1 Okhla Industrial Area,
New Delhi-110020

Author's Note

This book is mainly for the layman who would like to have an idea about Hinduism and the Indian way of life in the easiest way possible, without going into lengthy mythological treatises. It would be of special interest to the tourist who comes to India on a short visit. Since most of the miniature paintings, temple sculpture, and so on, are based on Hindu mythology, a basic understanding of the religion is necessary. My fourteen years' experience of interacting with tourists and giving them lectures on religion and history made me realise that the scope of the book had to include not just Hindu deities but also information on the Hindu way of life. The Miscellany Section answers questions on the sacred cow, marriage rituals, caste system, yoga, meaning of sectarian marks, karma, and describes many interesting things that a person would see on the streets of India.

The first section deals with the deities, where, illustrations have also been provided. The details of the festival connected with the deity are given at the end of each description, making it more meaningful. More festivals are mentioned in the 'Festival' section. One of the attractions of the book is the section on ancient Hindu sciences, music and dance with notes on painting and sculpture. Another helpful feature is the family tree of the deities which makes it easy for the reader to understand at a glance, the relationships of the various Hindu gods and goddesses and their incarnations.

I would like to thank my many friends for encouraging me in this venture. Prof. A. G. Kulkarni, Director, Science and Technology Centre, Jaipur, has been very helpful in going through the draft of the book, especially the section on science. Also to Kanwar Jai Singhji and Thakur Onkar Singhji for helping in the revision.

I am specially thankful to Raj Rana Hari Singhji, Mr Surojit Bannerjee and Mr. Krishan Kumar for giving very valuable suggestions.

I have attempted to keep the topics as simple and short as possible and would welcome comments and suggestions from readers.

TRAVEL WHEELS   DHARAM VIR SINGH
B 14 Bhawani Singh Road
Jaipur 302001, India

CONTENTS

MISCELLANY

FAIRS AND FESTIVALS

INTRODUCTION

It is hard to define Hinduism. It is not a religion in a narrow sense associated with the word religion. Its comprehensiveness bypasses the human mind. No single approach is able to enunciate its basic concept and philosophy. In a very broad sense, Hinduism is a way of life. From time immemorial, indigenous religious consciousness has continuously enriched it. It has been influenced by the aspirations and needs of the human society from time to time. It embraces the indigenous religions of India which have been modified almost continuously with the development of ideas and the needs of local communities. As a result, Hinduism is a mixture of sects, cults and doctrines which have had a profound effect on Indian culture. In spite of this diversity, there are a few of its aspects which do not rely in some way or the other on the authority of Indian religious literature - the Vedas, the Epics and the Puranas.

Vedic Deities

The Vedic gods who eventually became established in India may have been the result of the fusion of ideas brought by migrants and those of the indigenous people.

These deities were defined in the Vedas, along with meticulous descriptions of the ceremonies that were intended to propitiate them.

There is a popular school of thought which disputes the theory of the migrants having brought in ideas and is of the opinion that Hinduism was highly developed much before. It is, however, not within the scope of this book to go into this controversy.

It is evident from the Vedas that these deities were, to a certain extent, visualised as having human or animal forms. But it is not certain whether they were worshipped in the form of images. There remains the possibility, important for its effect on the later development of images, that some of the lower castes worshipped images in human or animal form and that this practice gradually spread upwards to the higher sections of society. At a much later period, the Vedic deities were given human form and reproduced as images.

In response to the forces of development, the old Vedic religion underwent several changes. These chiefly concerned the deities that were worshipped, and the forms of ritual. Some deities changed their function, or gained or lost popularity, while the powers of mediation between the deity and the devotee became monopolised by the priests (Brahmins) who alone could perform the necessary rites and rituals. This made the deities remote and some of them acquired awesome aspects. Consequently, while many of the old deities were relegated to minor positions in the pantheon, others were elevated, and new deities were introduced. Parallel with this, and as a possible reaction against the strict orthodoxy of the priests, the need gradually arose for a more satisfying relationship between the worshipper and the worshipped. This need for devotion (bhakti) towards a personal god stimulated the desire for images which would make the deity more approachable. Their introduction was a slow, uneven process and it is likely that images were made at first only of minor deities in the pantheon. One of the earliest references to images for worship is around the fifth century B.C. of the Yakshas (tree spirits) and Nagas (snake gods).

Epic Deities

Further stimulus to a more personal relationship between gods and men was given by the two great epics of Indian literature, the Ramayana and the Mahabharata. The stories of these epics are secular in nature but they not only describe the feats of their heroes but refer to the influence that the gods had on their exploits. Thus, the stories of the gods were supplemented and expanded as they were woven into the narratives and the heroes themselves got assimilated into Indian popular religion and became deified.

Puranic Deities

Further development of the Indian society brought about changes in religious concepts and an increase in the size of the pantheon. This grew by a process of absorption and combination, adopting popular (including female) deities into a sophisticated and well-developed assembly and merging several deities into one. Thus, the minor Vedic deity, Vishnu, was identified with Vasudeva

11

and another epic hero, Krishna. It is likely that the ten incarnations of Vishnu that eventually became conventional were attributed to him in a similar way.

Later, Krishna himself got assimilated with a pastoral flute-playing deity and became the subject of many poems and legends. At the same time, an ancient fertility god, Shiva, was elevated to the higher ranks of the pantheon and became an important deity with a variety of forms that gave him popularity equal to that of Vishnu. Shiva and Vishnu were visualised as forming a triad with Brahma. But, in spite of his ancient prestige, Brahma never received the widespread adoration enjoyed by the other two gods.

Beginning about fourth or fifth century A.D., attempts were made to create some sort of order out of the mass of myths and legends that had evolved around a large number of deities. Eventually these traditional tales were incorporated into the Puranas (ancient stories) summing up all that was known about the gods, with their elaborate genealogies, and providing religious instructions. In consequence, many of the deities who subsequently made their appearance are the result of formalisation given to them in the Puranas. At the same time, a further impetus was given to Hindu mythology (and thus a corresponding increase in the number of deities) by the development of Tantrism which emphasised the cult of the female partner (shakti) in association with a male deity, often Shiva.

From the fifteenth century onwards, a revival of interest in the bhakti movement brought about a widespread devotion to the cult of Krishna, one of the earliest gods to have human-like qualities.

The creative powers of India's religious life have not declined but continue with the same energy as they had earlier. For example, recently (in the 1960s), in Northern India, the goddess Santoshi Mata appeared complete with her own mythology and legends.

Why Do Hindu Deities Have so many Arms?

Image worship crept almost imperceptibly into Indian religions and was not only finally sanctioned in the religious scriptures, but, the images themselves, and the rituals for their worship were also described in greater detail. One of the results of this process, more especially the merging of two or more deities, was that some of the gods were shown as having several qualities.

The visual problem that this created for the sculptor or artist when he made images of the gods was solved by showing them with several arms. Each hand would hold some object which would symbolise or represent the various qualities of the particular deity. Some of the hands would be empty but the position of the fingers and the palms would signify the character of that god. For example, if the fingers are pointing towards the ground, it means that the god is of a charitable disposition, whereas, the fingers pointing upwards, as in a blessing, signify a protector (see illustration). These gestures (mudras) symbolised their individual powers and differentiated them from other deities.

Worship

Hindu worship (puja) is not congregational, except in sects which put great emphasis on devotion (bhakti). In the temple, the devotee may be present at fixed ceremonies or he may employ a priest to carry out a ritual for him, or summon the god's attention on his own. Puja varies with the size of the sect, the size of the temple etc. Domestic worship varies in accordance with the individual needs. A rich household may employ a full time priest while others may invite one to perform ceremonies on special occasions. One may also restrict himself to a prayer in the morning or in the evening, and may make an occasional visit to a temple on important festivals.

In a temple, normal religious observances are performed throughout the day: waking the deity in the morning followed by bathing, feeding and putting to rest at night. When entering the temple the devotee

rings a *bell* which is suspended from the ceiling at the entrance. This is done in order to shut out external sounds and to enable the devotee to make the mind go inward and concentrate. It also indicates the presence of the devotee in front of god. *Lights* are waved before the deity denoting that the Lord is "all light" and also as a mark of respect conveying the devotee's reverence. *Incense* is lighted to denote that the Lord is all-pervasive. The incense acts as a disinfectant also. The burning *of camphor* denotes that the ego should melt like it and the individual's soul should become one with the Supreme. The devotee offers *sweets,* rice, fruit, etc., to the Lord. These are then distributed among the members of the household or the devotees present at the temple. This is called *prasad.* The priest puts a red or yellow paste on the forehead of the devotee. This is called *tilak* and is applied on the forehead between the eyebrows at a point called the 'ajna chakra', indicating where the third or the spiritual eye is. This is not to be confused with the *bindi* mark which Indian ladies put on the forehead which is decorative or to indicate their marital status.

Circumambulation around the idol is done after the prayers. The idol is supposed to generate a halo, the advantage of which can be taken on going around it in a clockwise direction. Worship is of two kinds. The first is *saguna,* in which the worshipper uses a concrete symbol or idol which helps him to concentrate more easily. The second is *nirguna,* which is a higher step in which concentration is done on the Absolute by drawing the mind inward, without the help of any physical symbol to fix the mind on. In Hindu worship, it is not compulsory to go to a temple. One can meditate on the Absolute anywhere.

GodS
AND
GoddesseS

Brahma

Brahma has four faces, though only three can be seen. He has matted hair, wears a pointed beard and the eyes are usually closed in meditation. He has four hands which may hold a variety of objects such as a rosary, a water-pot, a book (the Vedas), a sceptre, a spoon, a bow or a lotus. Sometimes two of his hands may be in a boon-giving and protective mudras. His four faces represent the four Vedas and the four hands, the four directions. The rosary, which he is counting, represents time. The whole universe evolves out of water, therefore Brahma carries water in the water-pot.

He may wear a tigerskin or the skin of a black antelope as a garment and the sacred cord over his left shoulder. If coloured, he is pink or red. He is sometimes shown riding the goose, or sitting in the lotus position in a chariot being pulled by seven swans. The swan, which is the symbol of knowledge, is his vehicle.

In the Rig Veda the word Brahman (or Brahma) was used to indicate the mysterious power contained in sacred utterances. Later, this was associated with the skill of the priest who spoke the 'words' and he was described as a Brahmin. In the Upanishads, by a further development, this power was regarded as being universal and forming the elemental matter from which everything (including the gods themselves) originally emerged. Eventually, this supreme creative spirit became fully personalised under the name of Brahma.

Since this idea is linked with the origin of the universe, it was inevitable that Brahma should become associated with Hindu cosmogony. Many legends grew, particularly in the later texts, surrounding the connection with the origin and control of the universe. In one of them, the supreme soul and self-existent lord created the waters of the earth and deposited in them a seed, which became the golden egg, out of which He was born as Brahma. According to other texts, he became a boar who raised the earth from the primeval waters and thus created the world. He is described as assuming the appearance of a fish or a tortoise at the beginning of the ages. In much later developments of Hindu mythology these aspects are attributed to Vishnu, and Brahma assumes a secondary role. His worship slowly declined and has not been widespread since sixth century A.D.

Images of Brahma are still made. Many temples include one somewhere in their scheme of sculptural decoration, although it is only in extremely rare cases that he occupies the position of the main icon.

In the whole of India there are very few temples dedicated to Brahma. There is one at Pushkar, near Ajmer (Rajasthan), and another in Orissa.

In Hindu cosmology, the basic cycle which through the cosmos, passes through all eternity, is the Kalpa or the Day of Brahma, equivalent to 4320 million years. The night is of equal length, and 360 days and nights of this duration form one year of Brahma's life. This is expected to last hundred years.

VISHNU

Vishnu is blue coloured and has four or more hands. He is shown holding two of his most characteristic symbols: the wheel and the conch-shell. He is always clothed in yellow. The wheel represents the Universal Mind and the powers of creation and destruction that form the revolving universe. The conch-shell is associated with the origin of existence through its spiral form and its connection with water. Vishnu also holds the club which symbolises authority or the power of knowledge as the essence of life. He has an open upraised palm in the abhaya mudra, expressing reassurance. He sometimes holds a lotus and is also known as Narayan. His vehicle is Garuda (eagle) half-man, half-bird.

Vishnu is normally shown reclining on a bed made up of the coils of the serpent king, Sheshanaga, with Lakshmi/Shri, his consort, seated at his feet. Brahma is shown to have been born from a lotus springing from the navel of Vishnu. According to Hindu mythology, a cosmological substance is left over from the last age of creation from which a new cycle may be brought into existence. This is symbolised by the many-headed serpent king. Shesha means the leftover floating on the ocean which is thought to be like the Universe.

During the interval in the cycle of creation, Vishnu lies asleep on the coils of Sheshanaga, protected by its hood, until he is ready to begin a new cycle.

According to another creation story, Shesha was used as a rope (twisted around the world axis resting on a tortoise) with which the gods and the demons churned the waters of creation.

Vishnu is a striking example of the way in which the changing demands of religious life in India brought about changes in the status of deities, or the qualities they represented. Although Vishnu is mentioned in the Rig Veda, he became loosely associated with the sun and eventually, in the Mahabharata and the Puranas, he acquired a prestige that he has never lost. Ultimately he was invested with the qualities of permanence, continuity and preservation.

With the passage of time, Vishnu acquired the characteristics of several deities, including a number of popular folk ones, who were absorbed into the Vishnu cult in the form of incarnations. In the Mahabharata, he became identified with Krishna in his more martial aspects, but these were subsequently replaced by qualities of romantic love. Vishnu also took on the attributes of several deities in various animal forms such as the tortoise, the boar and the fish. It is likely that these developments took place slowly and were the result of the absorption of the cults that prevailed in different areas of India. Eventually, these diverse elements reduced and systemised into a group of twenty-four Vishnu incarnations. Some of the more common ones were used to form a small group of ten incarnations (avataras), viz. the Fish (Matsya), the Tortoise (Kurma), the Boar (Varaha), the Man-Lion (Narasimha), the Dwarf (Vamana), Parashurama, Rama, Krishna, Buddha and Kalkin.

Festival: Devuthani Ekadashi

Vishnu sleeps for four months, from June to July and from October to November. This four-month period is also the time when many of the other gods are sleeping and it is considered unlucky to perform any ceremonies during this period. When Vishnu and the other gods wake up, it is considered the right time to hold engagements and marriages. To celebrate the event, various ceremonies are held and in some places a cowdung-cake fire is lit and people gather around it singing hymns.

SHIVA

Shiva, the third god of the Hindu triad, has three eyes, the third one (between the eyebrows) being usually closed, except at the time of destruction of things. He wears long hair, supports the holy river Ganga on his head and the crescent moon on his matted hair. He has two to four arms, holds a trident in his hand, is naked except for a tiger-skin, besmears himself with ash and is decorated with snakes on his head, neck and arms. He is very fair-coloured but has a blue throat due to his having drunk poison during the time of the churning of the ocean by the gods. In his other hands he holds an axe, an antelope, and an hour-glass shaped drum called a 'damru'. He wears a garland of skulls and is also known as the lord of the cremation grounds. His consort is Parvati and he is the father of Ganesha and Skanda (Kartikeya). His vehicle is the bull called Nandi.

Shiva was not a Vedic god and in his earlier forms he was known as Rudra. In contrast to Vishnu's reputation as the benevolent creator god, Shiva represents destruction, austerity and the more malignant forces of life. This divergence has the effect that whereas Vishnu manifested himself through avataras, Shiva is represented by different aspects of his own powers and that of his consort.

His spiritual ancestor, Rudra, was ambiguous, being both benevolent and malevolent, and the latter aspect gradually prevailed. The combination of the ideas of creation and destruction is expressed in his late aspect as the

Supreme Being (Mahadeva). In this form he is frequently represented as the phallic symbol (linga) which is worshipped in a Shiva temple. The lingam can be said to represent the powers of regeneration and procreation.

Shiva is shown in many other forms also, having more than four arms. They are grouped as under:

Boon giving forms	six
Destructive forms	eight
Benign forms	twelve
General forms	twenty-eight
Dancing forms	eight (some books mention one hundred and eight different forms)

Festival: Shiva-ratri

Shiva-ratri (night of Shiva) is both a festival and a time to keep a vow. It is celebrated in February-March all over the country and devotees spend the entire night singing devotional songs in praise of Lord Shiva. The lingam is first washed with Ganga water and then milk, curd, honey, ghee (clarified butter), flowers, etc., are poured over it. Devotees, on this day, abstain from food, ending the fast with a meal of dates, fruits, nuts, sweet potatoes and beaten rice. Special celebrations are held at important Shiva temples at Chidambaram, Kalahasti, Khajuraho, Varanasi and Kashmir.

SHIVA: NATARAJA

Nataraja or the Dancing Shiva is a very popular image. It illustrates a legend in which Shiva, accompanied by Vishnu disguised as a beautiful woman, set out to subdue ten thousand holy men who were living in a nearby forest. The holy men became angry and invoked a fierce tiger out of a sacrificial fire but Shiva flayed it and wore its skin as a cape. Next, he was attacked by a poisonous snake but Shiva tamed it and wore it around his neck as a necklace. A dwarf was also sent on whom Shiva put his foot and performed a dance which was so brilliant that the holy men acknowledged Shiva as their master.

The symbolism of the dance, called Tandava, can be interpreted in many ways. It may show Shiva as the moving force of the universe and his five acts of creation, preservation, destruction, embodiment and release (of the souls of men from illusion). The last can be linked to the fire of the cremation ground, perhaps symbolised by the ring of flames round the dancer.

In the image of Nataraja, Shiva is caught in the middle of the dance with one foot on the dwarf and the other in the air. The dwarf is said to be the embodiment of ignorance, the destruction of which is the pre-requisite to enlightenment, true wisdom and release. Shiva's long hair fly out while he plays the drum. The drum indicates that God is the source of sound, the *Nada-Brahman*. The upper left hand carries the fire, the instrument for the final destruction of the universe. The lower right hand bestows protection. The lower left hand points to the left foot, showing that his feet are the sole refuge of the individual souls. The lifted foot stands for release from illusion.

FEMALE GODDESSES

Devi, or Mahadevi is the most complex and the most powerful of the goddesses. She owes these characteristics to the combination of her descent traced back to the great Mother Goddess of the ancient times and to shakti, the active dimension of the godhead, the divine power that underlies the godhead's ability to create the world and to display itself. Devi or shakti assumes both benign and terrible forms. In the benign forms she displays positive roles: fertility, the protection and establishment of religious order, cultural creativity, wifely duty and material abundance. Some important examples of these forms are Lakshmi, Saraswati, Sati, Parvati and Prithvi. In the terrible forms she plays her most fundamental protective role, guardian of the cosmos in the form of a formidable warrior. Besides supplicating the goddess for the bestowal of favours, her worshippers also invoke her for active and sometimes violent assistance against demons, terrors and disasters. This contributed to the development of a group of fierce-looking female deities.

Once female deities became fully independent they responded to the usual forces in Indian religion to take on different forms. They were made the vehicle for the assimilation of non-Hindu mythology and practices in the same way as their male counterparts.

Some goddesses have strong maternal natures, some are domestic and closely identified with male deities, some are the very embodiment of art and culture, some are associated with the wild untamed fringes of civilisation and there are also the ones who have strong independent natures and are great warriors. The number of goddesses in contemporary Hinduism alone is simply overwhelming. Apart from the innumerable village goddesses, there are also the geographical goddesses associated with specific regions. Some of the important groups of goddesses are the Nava-Durgas, the Sapta Matrikas and the Ten Mahavidyas.

THE NAVA DURGAS

The goddess Durga has nine important forms called the Nava-Durgas. During the Nava-Ratri festival (October), each of the goddesses is worshipped on a particular night for the destruction of evil and for the preservation of Dharma (religion). The nine Durgas are:

Shailputri – She is worshipped on the first night and is the daughter of Himavan. She has two hands, one holding a trident and the other a lotus. She rides a bull.

Brahmacharini – The second Durga-shakti has two hands. One holds a water-pot and the other a rosary. She symbolises devotion.

Chandraghanta – The third Durga-shakti is golden complexioned, rides a tiger and has ten hands and three eyes. The hands hold various types of weapons with two in a boon-giving and protective mode.

Kushmanda – The fourth Durga-shakti has eight arms, holding various types of weapons and a rosary. She rides a tiger and has a presence like that of the Sun.

 **Skandamata** – Riding a lion, she is the mother of Skanda who is shown sitting on her lap. She has three eyes and four arms with two holding lotus flowers and two in a blessing and protective mode.

Katyayani – The sixth Durga-shakti is the daughter of the sage Katya. Riding a lion, she has three eyes and eight arms holding various weapons. She is golden coloured.

 **Kalaratri** – She is black coloured with flowing hair, has three eyes and rides a donkey. She has four hands with two holding a cleaver and a torch.

Mahagauri – She is fair complexioned with four arms and wearing white clothes. She holds a drum and a trident and rides a bull. She has a peaceful expression on her face.

 **Siddhidhatri** – This form is shown seated on a lotus or a tiger. She has four arms and has the ability to bless her devotees with twenty-six different boons.

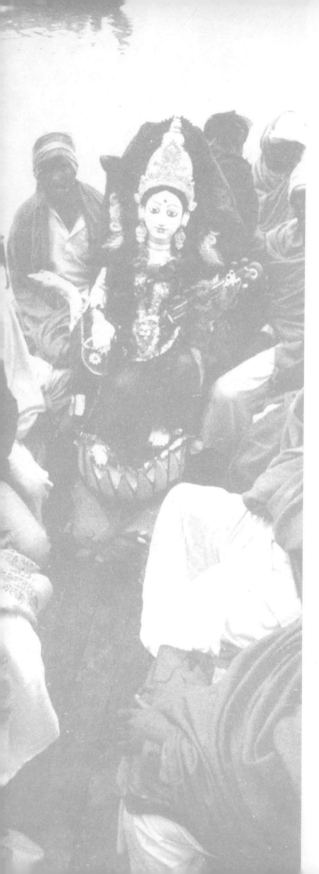

THE SAPTA MATRIKAS

The Sapta Matrikas, or seven Mother Goddesses, are primarily an independent group who have violent natures, are associated with diseases and are particularly prone to afflict small children. They have a single face and are recognised by their vehicle (animal/bird) shown with them. They usually have a small child sitting on the lap. The Matrikas are:

Brahmani has four hands, two carrying a vase, and a rosary and two in a boon-giving and protection pose. Her vehicle is a goose.

Maheshwari has four, six or ten hands, carrying a javelin and a rosary and two hands in boon-giving and protection poses. She has three eyes and the bull is her vehicle.

Kaumari has two, four or twelve hands, carrying a spear and a cock. Two of the hands are in boon-giving and protection poses. She has three eyes and rides a peacock.

Vaishnavi has four or six hands, carrying a conchshell and wheel. Two of the hands are in protective and boon-giving poses. She rides an eagle.

Varahi has a boar's head and four hands, carrying a plough and a spear and two in the boon-giving and protective poses. Her vehicle is the bull.

Indrani has four hands with two in the charitable and protective poses and two carrying a spear and a thunder-bolt. She rides an elephant.

Chamunda has four or ten hands carrying a skull-cap, a goad, a sword, a spear, an arrow, a shield, an axe, etc. She rides a corpse or owl.

THE TEN MAHAVIDYAS

The Ten Mahavidyas are an important group of female deities who are manifestations of the Supreme Goddess. They are not consistently described, and some of the goddesses, such as Kali and Tara are individually important and have several manifestations themselves. The following descriptions are typical of the way in which each of the forms is described.

Kali has a fierce countenance, is naked and dwells in the cremation grounds. She holds a severed head and a bloodied cleaver, has dishevelled hair, wears a garland of decapitated heads and a girdle of severed arms.

Tara is nearly identical to Kali. She is dark, rests her foot on a corpse, wears a tigerskin and a necklace of severed heads. She laughs terribly, stands on a funeral pyre and is pregnant. She has four hands holding a dish, a cleaver, a scissors and a lotus.

Chinnamasta stands in a cremation ground on the bodies of Kama and Rati. She has decapitated herself with a sword, which she holds in one hand. In the other hand she holds a platter with her head on it. Three jets of blood spurt from her neck and stream into the mouths of two female attendants and her severed head.

Bhuvaneshwari is said to nourish the three worlds. She has four hands with two holding a goad and a noose. She has a bright and light complexion and smiles pleasantly. Her large breasts ooze milk.

Bagala is sometimes shown as having the head of a crane, is seated on a jewel throne and is yellow skinned. In one hand she holds a club with which she beats the enemy and with the other she pulls out his tongue.

Dhumavati has a pale complexion and is tall, with a stern unsmiling expression. Dressed as a widow she wears dirty clothes, her hair is dishevelled, she has no teeth and her breasts are long and pendulous. She is afflicted with thirst and hunger, has a large crooked nose, a quarrelsome nature and rides a crow.

Kamala is described as a beautiful, golden complexioned woman surrounded by elephants pouring pitchers of water over her. She is seated on a lotus with two of the same flowers in her hands. She has an affinity to Lakshmi.

Matangi is coloured black. Her eyes roll in intoxication and she reels about like an impassioned elephant.

Sodasi is a girl of sixteen with a red complexion. She is shown astride the prone body of Shiva. They are on a pedestal supported by the gods Brahma, Vishnu, Rudra and Indra.

Bhairavi has a reddish complexion and wears a garland of severed heads. She holds a rosary and a book in two of her four hands, with the other two in a charitable and protective pose. Her breasts are smeared with blood.

Incarnations of Vishnu

Whenever the forces of evil began to rule the world, Vishnu, the great preserver, left the heavens and descended on earth in different forms to rescue mankind from evil. Vishnu is said to have taken ten incarnations, but, sometimes more than twenty-two forms are ascribed to him. Some of the forms are cosmic in character while some are based on historical events. It is interesting to note the evolution of these incarnations from lower to higher forms of life and their reflection on the history of the evolution of mankind. For example:

Matsya, the fish incarnation, symbolises the forming of protoplasm and invertebrates.

Kurma, the tortoise, symbolises the amphibian form.

Varaha, the boar, symbolises the existence of mammals.

Narasimha, the half-man half-animal incarnation, shows the development of hands and fingers on animals and the evolution of the sub-human or ape form.

Vamana, the dwarf, reflects the incomplete development of man.

Parashurama, the Rama-with-the-axe incarnation, symbolises the stone age. The axe symbolises the start of the use of metal by mankind.

Rama shows the ability of mankind to live in cities and to have an administration.

Krishna (one who knows the sixty-four arts), reflects the development of the sciences.

The **Buddha** incarnation reflects the intellectual and scientific development of man.

Kalki, in the years to come there will be a moral degradation in society and this future incarnation will save mankind.

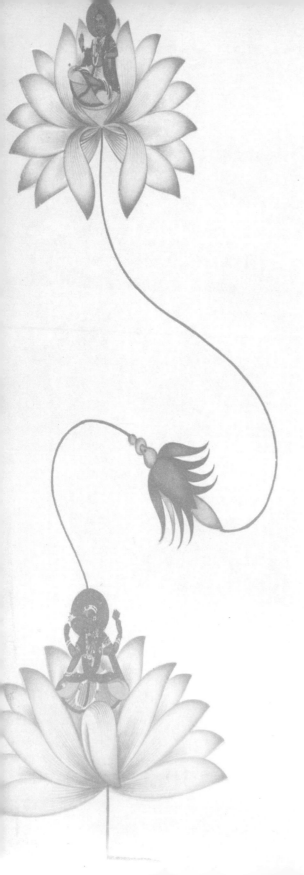

MATSYA

In his first incarnation, Vishnu has the lower part of his body like that of a fish (Matsya) and the upper part like that of a man. He has four arms; with two, he holds a conch-shell and a wheel, while the other two are holding a lotus or a mace or are in the protection and boon-giving modes.

There are several explanations as to why Vishnu assumed the form of the fish. One of them describes him as turning into a fish so as to be able to tow a ship in which Manu, the progenitor of the new human race, had taken refuge from a devastating flood. The same story is found in the Mahabharata where the fish is described as having a horn. In the Bhagavad-Purana, the story is further elaborated by the addition of a fight between Matsya and the demon Hayagriva, who had stolen the Vedas when Brahma was asleep.

KURMA

Vishnu, in his second incarnation, is in the form of half-man half-tortoise (Kurma). The lower half being the tortoise. He is normally shown as having four arms. In the upper two, he carries the conch-shell and the wheel while the lower two are in the protection and the boon-giving postures or carrying a mace and a lotus.

When the gods were in danger of losing their authority over the demons, Vishnu advised them to churn the ocean so that they might procure amrita (ambrosia) which would make them strong and immortal. He promised to become a tortoise on which would rest the mountain Mandara, which was used as the churning stick.

Together with ambrosia, the chu... ...face the other thirteen ob... ...they were, Lakshm... ...ra (the moon)... ...em for Vishnu... ...wish granting... ...ravata (the four... ...(the invincib... ...of the ambrosia... ...site, halahala (p... ...ind. The poiso... ...ing him the na... ...ng also brough... ...ot of ambrosia...

...one hand holding a mace and the other in a protective mode. There is the same conflicting account of this as of the two preceding incarnations, Matsya and Kurma. While some books describe it as an incarnation of Vishnu, others describe it as that of Brahma.

Vishnu turned himself into a boar (Varaha) and descended to the bottom of the ocean to rescue the earth which had been abducted and hidden there by a demon. After a long struggle, Vishnu (as the boar)

slew the demon, rescued the earth and brought it to the surface and made it ready to support life by modelling the mountains and shaping the continents. In this way, the world was once again brought into being to begin another kalpa or cycle. The extrication of the world from the deluge of sin is symbolised by this legend and is a creation myth.

NARASIMHA

Narasimha, the fourth incarnation of Vishnu, is in the form of half-man (Nara) and half-lion (Simha), having four hands. Two hands carry a wheel and a conch-shell and two are in the boon-giving and protection modes or tearing at the stomach of the demon-king. Vishnu assumed this form in order to overcome a demon king who could not be slain by a man or by a beast, either inside or outside a palace, by day or by night. Adopting the form of a lion-headed man, Vishnu approached the palace at dusk and hid himself in a pillar at the entrance, out of which he sprang and killed the demon-king, Hiranyakashipu. According to some scriptures the incident took place inside a pillar, while according to others Narasimha placed the demon on his lap and tore out his entrails.

The symbolism, here, is of the lion-like characteristics of fierceness, bravery and independence that claim almost universal admiration.

Festival: Narasimha Jayanti

Held in April-May, Narasimha Jayanti celebrates the killing of the demon king Hiranyakashipu by Vishnu in the form of Narasimha. People observe a fast and meditate on Narasimha on this day, and seek his blessings to have the qualities of devotion like that of Prahlad. People give to the poor on this day in charity.

VAMANA

The fifth incarnation of Vishnu is usually represented as a dwarf (Vamana) holding a water-pot in one hand and an umbrella in the other. He wears a ring of kusha grass on his third finger and occasionally carries a book. He has long hair, wears ear ornaments and covers his body with a deer-skin or loincloth. In his first four incarnations, Vishnu

appears in either an animal form or in a half-human half-animal form. The later incarnations starting from Vamana are all in human form. The first of them, Vamana, is perhaps significantly a dwarf, thus symbolising the underdeveloped stage of mankind.

The story of Vamana concerns Bali, the great–grandson of Hiranayakashipu. Bali's rule was so successful that his reputation began to overshadow that of Indra, who was obliged to seek Vishnu's help in order to regain his supremacy. Not wishing to use harsh measures against such a praiseworthy ruler, Vishnu resorted to a stratagem. He disguised himself as a dwarf and asked Bali to give him a piece of land three paces wide on which he could sit and meditate. Bali granted the request and Vishnu then used his supernatural powers to take possession of heaven and earth in two steps thus depriving Bali of his kingdom.

But, in recognition of Bali's generosity, Vishnu refrained from taking the third step and gaining the netherworld as well, but, installed Bali as its monarch. The story of Vishnu's dwarf is a creation myth symbolising the power of Vishnu to cover the universe.

Festival: Vamana Dwadeshi

Celebrated in August-September, the worship of Vishnu and Bali is recommended on this day. It is said that those who observe the day in due form and give freely to Brahmins, will be reborn as kings who will possess the celestial kingdom, like Bali.

PARASHURAMA

Parashurama is almost always shown with an axe in his right hand. He is also shown as having four hands carrying a battle axe, a sword, a bow and an arrow. In this, his sixth incarnation, Vishnu appears for the first time in a completely human form but, at the same time, he maintains his status as a deity.

As the story goes, a Kshatriya king had stolen Parashurama's father's wish-granting cow, Kamadhenu. Parashurama took his revenge for the theft by killing the thousand-armed king. But, in retaliation, the king's sons killed Parashurama's father. Vishnu took the form of Parashurama, not only to get revenge, but, to rid the world of oppression by the kings/Kshatriyas, which he did in the course of twenty-one battles. The story of this incarnation evidently points to a time in Indian history when there was a severe and prolonged struggle for power between the Kshatriyas and the Brahmins.

The story behind the name concerns the sage's son, Rama, a brilliant archer, who did penance in the Himalayas to Shiva in gratitude for having this skill conferred on him. Shiva was pleased with his devotion and when fighting broke out between the gods and demons, he ordered Parashurama to defeat the demons. Parashurama showed reluctance. Shiva then reassured him and he managed to defeat the demons. On completing the task Shiva gave Parashurama many gifts and weapons, including a magnificent axe (Parashu) after which he was known as Parashurama (Rama with the axe).

Festival: Parashurama Jayanti

On this sacred day, also known as Akshya Tritiya, apart from Parashurama, Lord Vishnu is also worshipped. Fasting, austerities and prayers are carried out by devotees on this day.

RAMA

Rama or Ramachandra, the seventh incarnation of Vishnu, is normally shown as standing, having two arms, in one of which he holds a bow. He usually has his wife Sita by his right side, holding a blue lotus. His brother Lakshman, shorter than Rama, stands by his left side, holding a bow and arrow. Hanuman, the monkey god, is usually shown kneeling a little in front and by Rama's right.

Though a comparatively minor incarnation whose task it was to kill a ten-headed demon, Ravana, who held his wife captive, Ramachandra has deeply influenced the Indian psyche and has risen to be a deity whose life is a subject for literature and an example of moral excellence.

As the hero of the great epic of India, Ramayana, he has also passed into the mythology of countries other than India whose cultures have been influenced by it. Rama is also considered a saviour and friend and is said to have the power of intercession for the dead. When a dead body is carried for cremation, the pall-bearers loudly repeat the words 'Ram nam satya hai' (Rama's name is truth). Rama represents the qualities of fidelity, gentleness and steadfastness. In the same way, his wife Sita (incarnation of Lakshmi, wife of Vishnu), is regarded as the embodiment of all that is most admired in Indian womanhood—faithfulness and affectionate compliance. They are looked upon as an example of constancy in marriage.

Festival: Ramanavami

Celebrating the birth of Rama, this festival is held in March-April all over India. At this time, temples dedicated to Rama are beautifully decorated with lights and flowers. Priests recite the Ramayana and highlight the important aspects of the life and character of Rama. The name of Rama is recited constantly as it is supposed to purify the heart.

KRISHNA

Krishna, the eighth incarnation of Vishnu, is considered the most important of the ten incarnations. He is usually shown as blue or black-skinned, having two hands and playing the flute. In paintings he is shown standing on one leg with the other crossed in front, resting on his toes. He usually wears colourful garments and is richly ornamented. He may hold a conch-shell or a curved stick in his hand. By his side would be his consort Radha and usually some cows (he was born as a cow-herd). In paintings he is shown as dancing with the cowherds and girls (gopis), as a child eating butter, or as Arjuna's charioteer addressing him in the battlefield.

Vishnu manifested himself as Krishna so as to kill the evil king Kansa. The king had been forewarned that the eighth child of Devaki would kill him, so he imprisoned Devaki and slaughtered her new born babies one by one. The seventh child, Balarama was saved by his kinsmen. When the eighth child was born, there was a big storm; the doors burst open, the guards fell asleep and Vasudeva (Krishna's father) walked out of the prison, taking the baby Krishna with him to Yashoda with whom he spent his childhood.

This incarnation of Vishnu has accumulated a great variety of myths. Krishna shows all the aspects of human development usually associated with childhood, adolescence and adulthood. There are few stages in a mortal worshipper's life, a counterpart of which cannot be found somewhere in the stories relating to the activities of Krishna. Although many of the stories about him concern his superhuman deeds, he also reveals human characteristics. The flute playing adds to the pastoral character of many of his stories and the effect it has on the gopikas provides a rich source of speculation on its symbolism which is apparent in a lot of poetry and in many dance forms, notably Kathakali in South India.

Why is Krishna Coloured Blue?

One of the theories is that Vishnu, because of his association with water, is depicted blue; therefore all his incarnations, including Krishna, are shown as such. In Hinduism, persons who have depth of character and the capacity to fight evil are depicted as blue skinned. Another theory refers to Vishnu implanting two hair, one black and the other white in Devaki's womb (which miraculously got transferred to Rohini's) and as a result, from the black hair Krishna took birth, with a dark skin, and from the white hair his brother, Balarama.

Festival: Janamashtami

Celebrating the birth of Lord Krishna, Janamashtami is held in August-September all over India. Temples are decorated, bells are rung, the conch-shell is blown and Sanskrit hymns sung in His praise. Devotees observe a fast for twenty-four hours which is broken at midnight, the time when Lord Krishna was born. The idol at that time is washed with milk and His name is chanted 108 times. In most places, particularly in Mathura and Brindaban, tableaux (jhankis) depicting episodes from Krishna's life are the highlights of the day. Special sweets are prepared for this festival.

BUDDHA

Buddha, the ninth incarnation of Vishnu, appears at the start of the present age. He has short curly hair and his feet and palms have marks

of the lotus. Calm and graceful in appearance, he is seated on a lotus flower. The lobes of his ears are shaped like a pendant and he is shown wearing a yellow robe. The hands are in a boon-giving and protection mode.

This incarnation is symbolic of the uneasiness that the Hindu priests felt for the Buddhists and their teachings which were becoming very popular with the masses. The Bhagvad-Purana says that 'as Buddha, Vishnu deludes the heretics'. As Buddha, Vishnu

advised the demons to abandon the Vedas, whereupon they lost all their powers and enabled the gods to establish their supremacy. The doctrines supposedly put forward by Buddha are far removed from Buddha's teachings as understood by his followers. Ironically, the Buddhists did in some sense turn to Hindu belief. The mythology and cosmology that became attached to Buddhism, as it became a popular mass religion, were rooted in Hindu belief and the Hindu gods inhabited some of the lower heavens of the Buddhist cosmos.

Festival: Buddha Purnima/Jayanti

It is celebrated in April-May. Three great events in Buddha's life on the same day has made Buddha Purnima the most important festival in the Buddhist world. It is celebrated all over the world with great piety, devotion and fervour. Buddha's images and portraits are taken out in a procession on this day.

KALKI

Kalki, the future and the last incarnation (avatara) of Vishnu, will appear at the end of the present age (Kali-yuga), when moral excellence would no longer exist, the rule of law would disappear and all would be darkness. Kalki would then ride forth on a horse, blazing like a comet and save mankind and re-establish Dharma or Righteousness. Kalki would usher in the Golden Age, a new era of purity and peace and then return to heaven.

In some texts Kalki is described as riding a white horse and holding a flaming sword. In others he is described as being four armed, holding a sword, a conch-shell, a wheel and an arrow. In still others, he is described as a horse-headed man carrying a club instead of an arrow. When riding a horse he sometimes carries a bow and arrow.

Agni

Agni, the God of Fire, is represented as a red coloured man having three legs, two to seven arms, dark red eyes, thick eyebrows and hair. In his hands he carries a spear, a fan, a cup and spoons and various implements used for fire associated ceremonies. He may have one or two heads and a pot-belly. Flames issue from his mouth with which he licks up the butter which the priest offers to the sacrificial fire. The priest, while pouring butter in the fire summons 'Svaha', the consort of Agni, by name.

He rides on a ram, wears a sacred thread, a garland of fruits and seven streams of glory radiate from his body. Agni is one of the few gods who have retained their supremacy in the Hindu hierarchy of gods, from the Vedic age till today, and has the largest number of hymns addressed to him. He is the priest of the gods and the god of the priests and serves as the liaison between gods and men. He presides over all the great events of a person's life and at the end it is Agni, through the flames of the funeral pyre, who accepts the body as an offering.

BALARAMA

The brothers, Krishna and Balarama were the sons of Vishnu and are sometimes regarded as his joint incarnations. Balarama is normally shown with two hands holding a club (gada) or a plough, and sometimes both.

According to the Vishnu-Purana, Vishnu took two of his hair, one black and the other white, and implanted them in Devaki's womb. Shortly before their birth they were miraculously transferred to Rohini's womb in order to prevent the infants from being killed by the tyrant king Kansa. After they were born, it was noticed that the complexion of Krishna was dark and that of Balarama, light. They grew up together, but, Balarama never became as popular as Krishna. Both brothers seem to have been the most human of all the incarnations. Neither had the saintliness that can be found in Rama and both displayed human weaknesses. In one incident, Balarama ordered the river Yamuna to move closer to him so that it would be more convenient for him to bathe, and when it did not, bullied it into doing what he wanted by threatening it with his plough.

Durga

Durga also is the consort of Shiva, Parvati being the other one. She is one of the most important female deities of the Hindus. She normally has eight arms and may hold any of the following items in her hands: a trident, a sword, a snake, a bell, a drum, a shield, a cup, a bow, a wheel, a conch-shell, a mace, an arrow and a water pot. She is shown seated in a 'sukhasana' (yogic posture) on a double lotus throne or on a tiger/lion. She may wear a garland of skulls.

Durga's relations with Shiva being sufficiently remote, she is worshipped in her own right. She is referred to as the 'shakti' of the Impersonal Absolute and as being worthy of worship for material gains in this world and spiritual advancement in the next.

Durga has nine popular forms, called Nava-Durgas, which are worshipped during the Dussehra festival. They are Shailputri, Uma/Brahmacharini, Chandraghanta, Kushmanda, Skandamata, Katyayani, Kalaratri, Mahagauri and Siddhidhatri.

Festival: Durga Puja/Dussehra

Symbolising the triumph of good over evil, Durga Puja or Dussehra is one of the chief festivals of India celebrated in September-October. It is celebrated in various parts of India in different styles, but, the one basic aim of this celebration is to propitiate shakti, the Goddess in her aspect as Power.

This is the festival in which the motherhood of God is emphasised. It is a ten-day festival, with each of the nine nights dedicated to different aspects of goddess Durga. Basically, the festival celebrates the victory of Durga over Mahishasura, the demon in the form of a buffalo. In many parts of India a buffalo is sacrificed to commemorate this event. The Devi temple in Tana (Chittorgarh) is famous for this festival.

In Northern India, on the tenth day, Dussehra is celebrated, signifying the victory of Rama over Ravana, whose effigies are burnt. Elaborate floats are also taken out in procession.

GANESHA

Ganesha has an elephant's head, four to ten arms, a pot belly, and is usually red or yellow in colour. His vehicle is a rat. In his hands he holds a rope, an axe, a goad, a dish of sweets, etc. The fourth hand is in a boon-giving position. It is said that with the axe Ganesha cuts off the attachment (to worldly things) of his devotees and with the rope pulls them nearer to the Truth.

A son of Shiva, he is one of the most popular gods and is called 'the remover of obstacles'. He is worshipped at the start of a ritual or the beginning of a journey. Endowed with a gentle and affectionate nature, he is also known as a god of wisdom. His images are found in practically every household and also on the outskirts of villages, as a guardian deity.

He is the Lord of the Brahmacharis (celibates). There are several accounts of Ganesha's birth. According to one, Parvati, wife of Shiva, created him from the scruff of her body to guard her door and when Ganesha refused to admit Shiva, the god cut off his head. On seeing Parvati distressed about this, Shiva promised to replace the head with that of the first living being he would chance upon. This happened to be an elephant. According to another account, Ganesha was conjured out of a piece of cloth by Shiva to produce a son for Parvati. Later, Shiva brought about the boy's death by decapitation, and then in order to placate Parvati, he called on the gods to find him a new head. After much searching they gave him an elephant's head. The tusk broke when it was cut from the elephant's body, therefore Ganesha is normally shown with a broken tusk.

The symbolism sometimes alluded to him is that his obesity contains the whole universe, his trunk is bent to remove obstacles and his vehicle, the rat, can creep through small holes to achieve the same goal, i.e., remove obstacles to reach religious ends.

Manifestations of Ganesha

According to the Ganesha-Purana, Lord Ganesha had four manifestations.

In the manifestation **Mahakota Vinayaka** he has ten hands, is riding a lion and is dazzling with brilliance. Shri **Mayuresh** has six hands, is fair complexioned and is riding a peacock. **Shri Gajaanana** has four hands, is riding a mouse and is crimson coloured. **Shri Dhoomraketu** has two hands, has a smoke-coloured complexion and is riding a horse. Another group of eight incarnations are:

(1) **Vakratunda**, riding a lion. (2) **Ekadanta**, (3) **Mahodara**, (4) **Gajaanana**, and (5) **Lambodara**, all riding a mouse. (6) **Vikata**, on a peacock. (7) **Vighnaraja**, riding on the serpent Sesha, and (8) **Dhoomra Varna**, like Shiva. Apart from the above, Ganesha has thirty-two other manifestations. Popular amongst them are **Vighnesh** (remover of obstacles), **Ekadanta** (the one-toothed one), **Modakpriya** (one who loves sweets), and **Ganapati** (head of the semi-divine Ganas). The most fearsome incarnation of Ganesha is that of **Vinayaka**, who is said to bring about catastrophe, madness and misfortune if he is displeased.

Festival: Ganesh Chaturthi

Ganesh Chaturthi (August-September) is observed all over India, particularly in Maharashtra, to celebrate the birth of Ganesha. A clay idol of Ganesha, sometimes eight metres high, is brought in the house, worshipped for two to ten days and then taken out in a procession and immersed in the sea or a lake. Coconuts and sweetened flour-balls are offered to him. Devotees are advised not to look at the moon on this day as it had behaved unbecomingly towards Ganesha once. The moral interpretation of this symbolism is that one should avoid contact with people who have no faith in God and religion.

GANGA

The Ganga is the most sacred of India's rivers. Goddess Ganga is represented as a fair-complexioned woman, wearing a white crown and sitting on a crocodile. She holds a water lily in her right hand and a lute in her left. When shown with four hands she carries a water-pot, a lily, a rosary and has one hand in a protective mode.

The story of Ganga's origin is indeed very interesting. Sagar, a king of Ayodhya, had no children. On doing a long penance he was promised, and got, sixty thousand sons. He then decided to perform a horse sacrifice. When Indra, the lord of the heavens, heard of this, he got scared and stole the horse and took it to the nether region. The sixty thousand sons reached the nether region after searching the earth for the horse and manhandled a sage by mistake, thinking he had stolen the horse. The sage, in anger, cursed them and turned them to ashes.

47

Sagar, on hearing this, prayed to Goddess Ganga to come down to earth and with her water to bring salvation to his sons.

His son and grandson also carried out the penance and it was only Bhagirath, the great-great-grandson, who managed to propitiate Ganga. The Goddess came down on earth in a rush, her impact being mitigated by being caught in Shiva's matted hair. She was led to the nether regions by Bhagirath. Hence, the Ganga is divided into three parts. One part, which remained in the heavens, was called Mandakini. The part that came down to earth is known as Ganga, and the part flowing in the nether region is called the Bhagirathi, named after the king Bhagirath.

Most of the holy cities of India are located on the banks of the Ganga. These are Rishikesh, Haridwar, Varanasi (Benares), Allahabad etc. Those who die within the specified limits of the Ganga go to the heavenly world. If, after cremation, the ashes are thrown into the Ganga, the same purpose is served. No Hindu would dare speak a falsehood with the Ganga water (Ganga-jal) in his hand.

HANUMAN

Hanuman, the monkey god, is a very popular deity and is worshipped all over India, specially in villages. His image is found in many forms, often with one head, two arms and a long tail looped over his head. He normally has a monkey's face on a very well built and strong human body. There are several other forms also, including one with ten arms and five heads. Apart from his own, the other heads are of a garuda (half-man, half-bird), a boar, a horse and a man-lion, representing the five most important avataras of Vishnu.

Hanuman is an important character in the Ramayana which depicts him as the epitome of devoted service and loyalty. His search for the heroine Sita, captured by Ravana, illustrates his superhuman powers and zealous performance of the tasks assigned to him. When he came to know that she was held captive in Lanka, Hanuman crossed the channel between India and Lanka with a giant leap. On being captured, he set Lanka on fire with his flaming tail and returned to Rama and helped him in many miraculous ways to besiege Lanka. Twice he flew to the Himalayas to collect medicinal herbs for his wounded companions. After the war, his wish to remain as Rama's faithful servant was granted. Every Rama temple has an idol of Hanuman as a minor deity. His worship is believed to destroy all evil.

Festival: Hanuman Jayanti

Held in March-April, Hanuman Jayanti (birth anniversary) is celebrated all over the country. People visit the temples where the idol is given a new coat of vermilion mixed with clarified butter and then richly decorated. Fasting is done and apart from the Hanuman Chalisa (hymn's of Hanuman), the Ramayana also is read. Tales of Hanuman's love for Rama are read aloud.

INDRA

Indra is the Vedic god of rain and thunder. He is also the king of the gods. He has four hands. In one hand he holds a thunderbolt, and in the others a conch-shell, a bow and arrows, a hook and a net. He is also shown as having two hands and eyes all over his body, and is called 'the thousand-eyed one'. His mount is the king of the elephants, Airavat, who is white in colour and has four tusks.

In the earlier Vedic period, Indra was very powerful and was shown as the protector of cows, priests and even gods. There are more hymns in praise of Indra than in the praise of other Vedic gods. He has a beautiful consort, known as Indrani. In the post-Vedic period and during the age of the Puranas, Indra fell from the front rank of gods and was given a status lower in all respects. Though still the king of the smaller gods, he is inferior to the holy triad of Brahma, Vishnu and Shiva. At a later stage, he is described as the ruler of Swarga (heaven) where the gods live. At this stage he is shown as having developed human frailties.

Though not the object of direct worship in temples, he constantly appears in the tales of religious scriptures. His idol, sitting on an elephant, appears on the walls of many Vishnu temples. Indra is also the guardian of the East.

KAMADEVA

Kamadeva, the god of love, is very fair and handsome and the best looking among the gods. He carries a bow made of sugarcane and strung with a line of humming bees. He shoots with his bow the five flower-tipped shafts of desire . He is accompanied by his wife Rati (passion) and his friend Vasanta (spring), who selects for him the shaft to be used on the current victim. Kamadeva's vehicle is the parrot.

Generally described as the son of Lakshmi and Vishnu, he is also said to be the son of Brahma. Surrounded by beautiful nymphs (Apsaras), he loves to wander around specially in springtime, loosing his shafts indiscriminately, but with a preference for innocent girls, married women and ascetic sages. Shiva burned him to ashes as punishment for disturbing his deep meditation, but Kamadeva's shaft had gone home and Shiva could not obtain peace until he had married Parvati. During all this time, Kamadeva lay dead and love disappeared from the earth. At length Shiva allowed him to be born as the son of Krishna. The god of desire, thus, fittingly became the son of the other deity in the pantheon associated with love.

Kartikeya

Kartikeya, the god of war and general of the army of gods, is known for his extraordinary strength. He is yellow skinned and usually has six heads. Depending on the number of arms depicted, he holds in his hands, a spear, a bow, an arrow, a noose, a discus, a cock, a shield, a conch-shell, a plough and a sword. He has one hand in a charitable and the other in a protective pose. In many idols, found in the Southern part of India, he is shown as having twelve arms. His vehicle is the peacock.

His origin may have resulted from the assimilation of a deity from the Southern parts of India. In ancient times, his worship was very widespread and there are references about his images in homes and temples.

With the advent of Shiva, Kartikeya started losing his importance in Northern India where he was sometimes relegated to the position of a guardian deity in Shaivite temples. In the South, he is still popular, and is also associated with deities like Murugan, Velan and Seyyon. In some texts, he is regarded as the son of Shiva and Parvati and is therefore the brother of Ganesha. The reason for his having six heads can be found in one of the stories relating to his birth. A passage in the Mahabharata mentions Agni's adulterous relationship with six wives of the Rishis (ascetics), who represent the six stars that form the Indian Pleidaes in the constellation of Taurus. The relationship resulted in the birth of Kartikeya. Because of his having six heads, all his six mothers were able to suckle him at the same time.

Festival

In the Hindu month of Kartik (October-November), the clay image of Kartikeya is worshipped and then immersed in the river. At the festival associated with the goddess Durga, his image is set up by her side. Many women worship Kartikeya so that they may be blessed with a male offspring.

KUBER

Kuber is the god of wealth and the gods' treasurer. His white body is dwarfish. He has three legs and eight teeth. He has two to four hands and may carry in his hands a mace, a purse containing money, a vase, a fruit and a bowl, and two hands in the boon-giving and protective modes. If shown as having two hands, he will carry a bowl and a money-bag.

His body is covered with jewels and other ornaments. For moving about he has a chariot called Pushpak. Kuber is not an important deity and his images are very rarely seen, though he is frequently referred to in the epics. He is also called the god of the Yakshas (savage beings). His brother Ravana, by practising austerities, obtained from Shiva the boon of invincibility and so was able to defeat Kuber and seize and retain Lanka and the chariot, Pushpak. As Lanka could not be restored to Kuber, Viswakarma, the architect god, built him a palace on Mount Kailash. He also has a beautiful garden called Chaitrarath on Mount Mandara. Kuber's domains are all in the high Himalayas, partly because he is the guardian of the North, but, also because the mountains are the repository of mineral wealth. Kuber watches over the earth's storehouse of gold, silver, jewels, pearls and the nine nidhis, special treasures.

LAKSHMI

Lakshmi is the consort of Vishnu and the goddess of wealth and good fortune. She normally has four arms when worshipped on her own, but has two when shown with Vishnu. She may hold a lotus in each of her upper hands. Gold coins can be seen dropping down from the palms of her lower two hands or one of them may be in a boon-giving posture. She is normally painted in a bright golden colour and is shown seated or standing on a lotus. In paintings, she is sometimes shown with two elephants, half submerged in water, one on each side. Lakshmi was born from the churning of the oceans by the gods for ambrosia.

Lakshmi is also associated with beauty and is one of the most popular Hindu female deities. It is likely that, because of the underlying human desire for wealth, she absorbed a large number of folk elements during her evolution into a widely accepted member of the pantheon. Some of these may be discerned in the qualities attributed to her as Vishnu's wife in several of his incarnations. As Sita (Rama's wife) she was said to have been born from a furrow, showing her link with agriculture. This symbolism is again emphasised when she is called Earth (Dharani), the wife of Vishnu.

Festival: Diwali

Diwali, the festival of lamps (October-November), is associated with Lakshmi and is celebrated all over India. During the festival, little lamps are lit all over the house in the belief that wealth (Lakshmi) will not enter a house if it is dark. Every city, town and village is turned into a fairyland with thousands of flickering oil lamps and electric lights illuminating homes. This is also the time when all houses are thoroughly cleaned and freshly painted, rice-flour designs are made on the doorsteps and crackers burst by children. The new commercial year for Hindu businessmen begins with Diwali.

Nandi

Nandi (the bull) is the vehicle (vahana) of Shiva and is normally found in all Shiva temples, either near the idol or facing it from a distance. It is also placed at the entrance of Shiva temples in a sitting or standing posture.

In paintings he is shown pure white. He has a rounded body, large brown eyes, heavy shoulders, a shining coat and a black tail. The hump is like the top of a snow-capped mountain. He has a golden girth round his body and sharp horns with red tips.

Originally, under the name of Nandikeshvara, Nandi seems to have existed in human form as a sage (rishi) who acted as Shiva's door keeper before achieving divine status. The reason for the association may have stemmed from Shiva's relationship with Rudra, who was sometimes referred to as the bull. This probably has roots in the vast mythology and the symbolism surrounding bulls that are found in ancient cultures. Nandi's association with fertility is illustrated by the custom of the devotees touching the feet and testicles of the Nandi idol when entering a Shiva temple.

Parvati

Parvati, the consort of Shiva, is represented as a fair and beautiful woman, with no superfluity of limbs. Few miraculous deeds are claimed for her. It is only when she appears as Durga, Kali, etc., that she manifests divine powers and exhibits a very different spirit.

As Kali, she became an ascetic whose severe penances were intended to attract the attention of Shiva. When Shiva teased her about her dark skin, through penances she had her colour changed to that of gold and was then called Gauri.

Parvati is not important enough to be worshipped alone but only as a minor deity in a Shiva temple. Between the fifth and the thirteenth centuries, from being merely the consorts and active partners of the male deities, female deities (shakti) became independent and objects of worship in their own right having a temple in which they were the main icons. It was around this time that Parvati, from a minor deity as a consort of Shiva, became a major deity as Durga and Kali. When Parvati is shown alone, she may hold a javelin and a mirror in her two hands. If she is four handed, two of her hands exhibit the protection and boon-giving attitudes and two carry a javelin and a chisel.

In the illustration facing this page, Parvati is seen doing a penance to attract the attention of Shiva.

Saraswati

Saraswati, the goddess of learning and knowledge, is represented as an extremely beautiful woman with a milk-white complexion. She normally wears white clothes, sits or stands on a water lily and has four arms. With one of her hands, she is presenting a lotus to her husband, by whose side she constantly stands, and in the other she holds a book of palm leaves indicating learning. In one of her left hands she has a string of pearls and in the other she may hold a small vase or the hand may be in a boon-giving pose. She is also represented with two arms, playing a stringed musical instrument called the Veena. She may also hold a conch, a wheel, a noose, a skull cap, a cup of ambrosia, a goad and a mace.

She presides over and protects the arts and is credited with the invention of writing. She is also the goddess of speech, the power through which knowledge expresses itself. In the Vedas, Saraswati is primarily a river, but in the hymns, she is celebrated as both a river and a deity. Her origins are obscure but it is possible that she once had something to do with the river Saraswati in Rajasthan or with water in some other way. At all events, she seems to have been associated with the creative properties that water has for seeds and vegetation. Being the goddess of learning, she is worshipped when a child is given instructions for the first time in reading and writing. Many schools in India start classes with a mass prayer to the goddess.

Festival: Saraswati Puja/Vasant Panchami

Saraswati is worshipped inJanuary-February when musical instruments, pens, paint brushes and books are cleaned and placed on an altar. These are devoutly worshipped as being the abode of the goddess. In the absence of an image, an ink pot or flowers are placed on a book and prayers from the scriptures are chanted.

Soma

Also known as Chandra, Soma (Moon) is identified with amrita (nectar). He is represented as a copper-coloured man, trailing a red pennant behind his three-wheeled chariot, which is drawn either by an antelope or by ten white horses. He normally has two hands, one carrying a mace and the other in a protective mode. His lineage says that he was the son of Dharma or of Varuna, lord of the oceans, from which the moon rises.

According to a legend, Surya nourishes the moon with the water from the ocean when Soma is exhausted by the many beings who feed upon his substance. For, during half the month, thirty-six thousand divinities feed on Soma and thus assure their immortality. This account neatly combines the two aspects of Soma: as the nectar from which the gods derive their strength and as the moon which waxes and wanes. The legend of the banishment of Soma by Brahma to the outer atmosphere can be interpreted as yet another myth explaining how intoxicants came to be banned.

Surya

Surya (the Sun god) is one of the most important deities of the Vedas. He usually has a lotus in each hand and is shown in a chariot drawn across the heavens by seven horses or one horse with seven heads. He is also shown with four hands, three carrying a wheel, a conch-shell and a lotus and the fourth in a protective mode. His charioteer is Aruna, the god of dawn, who carries a whip in his hand.

Being the source of light and warmth, he has the ability to control the seasons and the power to grant or withhold the ripening of the crops. As the economy was agricultural based, Surya is placed amongst the highest of the gods, specially for the agricultural communities.

Also known as Savita, Surya was very popular in the early times, but later on lost some of his importance to Vishnu. Nevertheless, he is the god to whom the famous Gayatri Mantra (prayer) is chanted everyday when he rises. Every morning one can see hundreds of devotees chanting the mantras and offering water to the Sun god. Small images and visual representations of the Sun god can be seen in the temples of other gods, but he rarely has a full-fledged temple to himself. One of the exceptions is the famous sun temple at Konarak in Orissa.

Varuna

Varuna, the god of the oceans, is shown as a fair-complexioned man riding a monster fish called Makara, which has the head and legs of an antelope. He may have two to four hands and in one of his right hands he carries a noose.

Varuna lost his importance during the Vedic times. Of his former character of a celestial deity, he retains only the title of the regent of the Western quarter of the compass. The mythological explanation of this great fall is that a great conflict occurred between gods and demons and when it was over, each of the gods was assigned a clearly defined sphere of influence to avoid further conflicts. From this time onward, Indra remained god of the atmosphere while Varuna was ousted from the guardianship of the heavens and was given the over-lordship of the oceans. Here he kept watch over the various demons of the ocean. Varuna sits with his wife, Varuni, on a throne of diamonds and the gods and goddesses of the different rivers, lakes and springs form his court.

Vayu

Vayu is the god of the wind. Extremely handsome in appearance, he moves about noisily in a shining chariot drawn by a pair of red or purple horses. At times the number of horses increase to forty-nine or even a thousand. The latter number would probably be employed when there is a cyclone. He is also represented as a fair-complexioned man riding a deer and carrying a white flag. He may have two to four hands and may carry a goad and a wheel.

Often associated with Indra, Vayu won the race for the first draught of Soma juice (ambrosia). He does not occupy a very prominent position in the Vedic hymns. He is considered the friend of the waters. At a later stage he is said to have begotten a son, Hanuman (the monkey god), who played a conspicuous role in the epic Ramayana. In the other epic, Mahabharata, Bhim also is said to be the son of Vayu.

Vishwakarma

Vishwakarma is the divine architect of the whole universe and is normally shown as white coloured. He normally has four hands carrying a water-pot, a book and a noose. He may hold craftsmen's tools in one of his hands or they may be shown placed near his seat. He has a club in his right hand, wears a crown, a necklace of gold, rings on his wrists and holds tools in his left hand.

All the flying chariots of the gods, their weapons, etc. were his creations. He built the city of Lanka for Ravana, and Dwaraka, the city associated with Krishna. It was he who revealed the science of mechanics and architecture (Satapatya Veda). According to Satpatha Brahmana, he performed a yagna in which he offered all creatures including himself, as sacrifice, to elucidate the cyclic process of destruction and renewal of all cosmic life and matter.

His daughter Sanjana was married to Surya, the Sun god.

Vishwakarma is the presiding deity of all craftsmen. Implements of the trade such as lathe machines, chisels etc. are worshipped when the Sun enters the Bhadrapada constellation. Jaipur has an industrial area named after him, and so are thousands of machining and mechanical shops all over the country.

YAMA

Yama is the messenger or god of death and the judge of men. He is represented as a green coloured man, clothed in red garments and wearing a crown. He wears a flower on his head, carries a mace in one hand, and a noose in the other for catching his victims. He is sometimes shown as having four arms and sometimes two. His mount is a black buffalo.

The twin brother of Yami, who later became the river Yamuna, he was the first mortal to die and having discovered the way to the other world, is the guide of those who depart this world. He has two ravenous dogs, each with four eyes and wide nostrils. They guard the road to his abode and wander amongst men summoning them to their master. In the Puranas, Yama is called the judge of men who, when

they die, are brought before him and Chitragupta (the Record Keeper) with whom their actions have been recorded. The virtuous are conveyed to heaven (Swarga) and the wicked to different regions of hell (Naraka). After death, the soul takes four hours and forty minutes to reach Yama. Therefore, a dead body should not be cremated before this time has elapsed.

Brahma, after creating the world, realised that a place for judgement and punishment for the wicked was wanting. He therefore requested Vishwakarma, the architect god, to create one. This legendary place created for Yama has a mild and salubrious climate and there is no fear of enemies or any affliction of mind or body. Each person is rewarded according to his past deeds. To the virtuous and to the sinner, Yama appears in different forms. To the virtuous he appears like Vishnu, with a charming, smiling face and lotus-like eyes. To the wicked, he appears to have limbs 'three hundred leagues' long, hair like gigantic reeds and eyes like deep wells. Yama is also the guardian of the South.

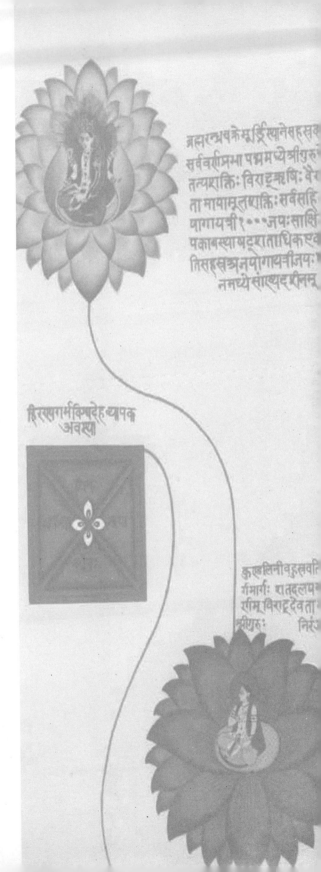

THE WEEKLY DEITIES

Ravi-var (Sunday) is the day of the Sun. He is red coloured and rides a one-wheeled chariot pulled by seven horses. He is shown with two to four hands carrying two lotus flowers or a wheel and a conch-shell. Sunday is the day to worship Shakti (Female Energy) and a good day to begin a new venture. Red colour should be worn on this day.

Som-var (Monday) is the day of the moon, a white coloured deity riding a three wheeled chariot and carrying a mace in one hand. The chariot is pulled by three horses. A person born under his influence will be honourable, powerful and rich. One should undertake a fast and wear white on this day.

Mangal-var (Tuesday) is ruled by Mangal who is red coloured and rides a ram. He has four arms and carries a trident and a mace. He sometimes rides a chariot. Mangal being malefic, the deity should be propitiated so that he may refrain from malevolent activities. A king starting a war on this day will be victorious. No auspicious activities should be started on this day and one should wear red for good-luck.

Budh-var (Wednesday) is the day of Mercury (Budh). He is the son of Soma (Moon), light yellow in colour with four arms carrying a mace, a sword and a shield and riding a lion. The clothes and garland worn by Budh are also yellow coloured. He is considered wise and always exerts an influence in conjunction with other planets. Feeding brahmins on this day is considered good.

Brihaspati-var (Thursday) is also called Guruvar. A yellow coloured deity, he normally sits on a lotus or a golden chariot pulled by eight horses. He is four armed and holds a mace, a rosary and a sphere in his hands. A person under his influence will have a lot of wealth. A girl coming to motherhood on this day will have many sons. Brihaspati is the teacher of the Gods. Thursday's colour is yellow.

Shukra-var (Friday) is the day of Shukra, the teacher of the demons. He is white coloured and sits on a lotus. He is also shown riding a chariot with lots of flags and being pulled by eight flame-coloured horses. He has four hands with two holding a rosary and a mace. He is the most auspicious of the planets. It is good to fast on Fridays.

Shani-var (Saturday). Shani (Saturn) is the most malicious of the planets. He is a black coloured old man riding a vulture or an iron chariot. He is shown with four hands holding a bow, a trident and an arrow. All misfortunes are traced to him, so much so that periods of misfortune are termed as 'Shani-dasa'. Due to a curse given by his wife, Shani has the capacity to cause destruction with his eyes. Hence, he is always looking down so as not to destroy anything. The planet should be worshipped on Saturdays to reduce his evil influence.

MISCELLANY

AUM / OM

The eternal, mystical syllable—the syllable that stands for the whole universe. It is pronounced with a nasalised ending, halfway between M and N. The letters comprise a triangle that physically delineate all the possibilities of sound. This sacred word encompasses in itself the whole universe, the past, the present and the future and  goes beyond the periphery of Time itself. Beyond the symbol of the Brahman or the Universal Soul, it is the very essence of all that is sacred in Hindu thought. It is used at the beginning of meditation, at the beginning and at the end of a prayer, during the practice of yoga, in fact, at all times when the thought of the Brahman pervades one's being.

AHIMSA

Ahimsa means non-injury, not harming or wishing to harm any being. It is the cornerstone of traditional Indian ethics and especially prominent in Jain doctrine and the teachings of Mahatma Gandhi. Ahimsa is the essence of compassion and humane nature. It advocates positive practices that may include vegetarianism, cow and animal protection and non-violence. The yogi begins the journey of enlightenment by perfecting his conduct through five restraints, of which the first is Ahimsa. The great gods of Hinduism are believed to love and aid all beings, their devotees strive to emulate that model. The ancient sage Vyasa stated, "Ahimsa means not to cause any pain to any creature, by any means or at any time. The restraints and disciplines that follow have their roots in Ahimsa and tend to perfect Ahimsa". Ahimsa is personified in Hinduism as the wife of Dharma (Righteousness).

ASHRAMA

In classical India, a remote hermitage of an ascetic or teacher which is a centre for religious study and practice is called an ashrama. It may be a simple place where the guru and his disciples reside. It may also mean a Hindu equivalent of a monastery or hermitage and may be highly complex with schools for religious education, guest houses, medical care and a host of charitable enterprises. The ashrama is dependent on voluntary contributions from individuals and rich business communities. Commonly at any ashrama it is the guru who is all important. He would lead an austere and disciplined life of meditation, study and instruction. In Hindu mythology, such habitations are frequently depicted in Utopian terms as places where wisdom and Dharma flourished.

ATMAN

Atman is that part of the living being that is eternal and beyond physical description. It is the true Self, the eternal soul that dwells within but has no personal characteristics. Atman is the birthless, deathless reality that is at once the innermost being of each person and the inmost being of all that which exists. Atman, more fully, is 'that which pervades all; which is the subject and which knows, experiences and illuminates the subjects and which remains always the same'. In many of the Upanishads, the meaning of atman is uncertain, since it may designate either the supreme and transcendent spirit or the finite individual self of man. According to Vedanta philosophy, the atman is of the same nature as the Universal Soul (Brahman), and as such seeks union with it in mystical liberation (Moksha).

BHAGAVAD GITA

The Bhagavad Gita is the most popular and sacred book of the Hindus and is widely known and read all over the world. An integral part of the Mahabharata, it stands as an independent work consisting of a dialogue between Krishna, the eighth avatara of Vishnu, and the noble warrior Arjuna. The latter is about to enter into battle against his cousins, an act he considers reprehensible and immoral, and seeks an answer from Krishna.

The Gita, as it is popularly called, is composed of eighteen chapters. The basic core narrates Arjuna's doubts whether it would be proper for

him to fight and thus become guilty of bringing about the ruin of his family and of law and order. Krishna replies that he should carry out his duty, because all human beings are but instruments in the fulfillment of God's eternal designs. This point he makes by revealing himself as the Supreme in all His glory and power. As the mortal Krishna again, he delivers a philosophical summary concerning pure and impure knowledge, pure and impure wisdom, and the nature of Karma.

The Gita belongs to a long age of changing sociological conditions, from that of the priestly Vedic world, centred upon the sacrificial fire in which the perfect observance of ritual was essential to salvation, to that of the world of kings, courts, warriors, princes, armies and battles, and forest sages and teachers. It is a great exposition of the doctrine of Bhakti, devotion to God, as well as of Gyan, the ultimate knowledge of the Supreme.

Rather than salvation gained through the offices of the priests, salvation came by attention to duty and the recognition of past acts upon which the present and the future are based. The individual's attitudes towards God are given a new direction: in place of knowledge (as exemplified by scholars as 'the way'), the individual may reach and become merged in God through his loving devotion or Bhakti, a way that was to develop into a widespread movement encompassing people at all levels and eschewing caste rules.

The scene for the working out of the Gita is a battlefield near Delhi where the battle between the Kauravas and the Pandavas, involving an army of five million, took place and continued for eighteen days. Some scholars have dismissed a literal war and state it is nothing but an allegory, in which the battlefield is the soul and Arjuna is man's highest impulses struggling against evil. Scholars and thinkers from many parts of the world have written commentaries on this Book of Knowledge from ancient times to the present and yet it reveals ever-new dimensions and interpretations.

BHAKTI

Bhakti is an expression of love, devotion and faith centred upon the Supreme Person rather than the Supreme Abstraction. It became a popular folk movement which was very strongly opposed by the Brahmins as it disregarded traditional Vedic rituals, ignored caste differences and placed devotion over knowledge. The Bhagavad Gita is the first major expression of Bhakti which, over the centuries, spread throughout the country through the wandering holy men and sadhus. It became the religion of the great masses of India for it enabled the individual to approach the Divine directly and become part of His all-encompassing love.

One of the underlying themes of Bhakti is that of incarnation (avatara), God manifesting himself upon the earth in some form (animal or human) in order to aid mankind in times of trouble. Krishna is the supreme example as the manifestation of Vishnu.

THE CASTE SYSTEM

Caste is a term applied to social groups in India which rank in a hierarchic order and within which there is a minimum of social mobility. The word 'caste' first appeared as a term 'casta' by which the Portugese travellers of the fifteenth century referred to the division of Indian society. The caste system may have its origins in the distant past when the Indo-Aryans invaded the country and instead of destroying the local inhabitants after the conquest, they absorbed them into their society by giving them a lower but definite place. This was the birth of the caste system which later on had four levels viz., the Brahmins or the priestly class, the Kshatriyas or warriors, the Vaishyas who followed commercial occupations and the Sudras who performed manual labour. In the beginning this division was based on performance, but later, it came to be determined by birth.

In course of time the 'jatis' or sects became more important than the castes. They were mainly occupational (like the goldsmith jati) and served the purpose of guilds which protected the interests of the members. Eventually, these jatis or sects grouped themselves under the main classes. The sects were very rigid and did not permit fluidity of movement, even where old occupations had broken down and new ones come into being. This rigidity had a disadvantage as it prevented the interaction and absorption of new ideas in the various trades and occupations.

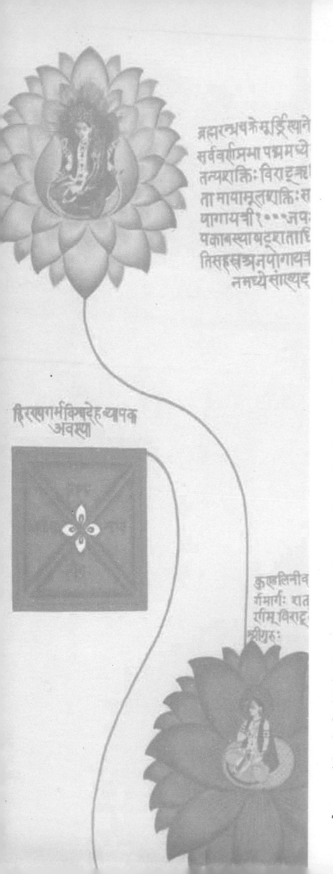

The 'untouchables' or 'outcasts'—there is no religious sanction whatsoever in Hinduism to the concept of untouchability, although later additions on the subject were inserted in the scriptures to justify its existence. It was a purely social practice introduced by the upper castes to provide themselves with menial labour to perform tasks repulsive to themselves, such as cemetery keeping, scavenging, etc. People breaking caste rules were sometimes made outcasts.

The upper castes tried to prevent inter-caste marriages as well to prevent the upward movement of the lower castes. Towards this end, the Brahmins, for example, tried to make the knowledge of the scriptures their monopoly and the rituals more and more elaborate so that only they could interpret them, whereas the Vaishyas attempted to become the only custodians of the wealth of the land, and the Kshatriyas considered only themselves eligible for ruling and governance.

With the start of the foreign invasions in the eleventh century, when life, property and the chastity of women were of little value to the invaders, the caste system became more rigid and protective, and each community built a fortress of social norms around itself. For example, the guarding of the sanctum sanctorum in temples which only a few could enter, child marriages (before a girl could be of an age attractive enough to be abducted by the invaders) etc., became the norms during those unsettled times in Indian history.

With the spread of education, the caste system is now dying out and any discrimination on the grounds of caste is punishable under the laws of the land.

CHAKRA

Chakra has two meanings. In the first meaning, it symbolises the universal law and its reflection in the moral law of man; the focus of spiritual power in human consciousness; the universal sun and the inner light of illumination. In a mystical sense, in tantric yoga, it is a centre of the body. There are six major chakras, namely, muladhara (base of the spine), svadhisthana (pubic region), manipura (midriff), anahata (solar plexus), visuddha (base of the neck) and ajna (between the eyes). The

ajna chakra is also known as the third eye. The chakras run in a line from the centre of the pelvis to the ajna. Above these chakras there is still another mystical centre, the sahasra-padma, at the top of the skull, which is sometimes counted as the seventh chakra.

Each chakra contains a lotus, the petals of which represent different mystical and religious qualities, and are the seats of various deities. The goddess Devi (or Kundalini, the serpent power) is coiled around the muladhara, and when properly awakened in tantrism through yoga, ascends in force to the sahasra-padma. It requires constant efforts at inner reflections in order to obtain this level of sadhana.

The ajna chakra indicates the level of the plexus and whose real operative part is at the back of the head where the little brain (cerebellum) joins the large brain (cerebrum). This sounds quite logical also when we consider the two functions of the brain which regulate the conscious and the subconscious minds. This coincides with the description of the ajna chakra as a lotus with two petals.

The ruling deities of all the chakras are different forms of Shiva and Shakti (female energy) and it is at the ajna chakra that they are united as one into 'ardha-narishwar', a manifestation of Shiva which is half-male and half-female. This symbolises the unification of the two minds and the two states of consciousness.

COLOUR IN HINDUISM

Colours play a very important role in the Hindu religion and culture and have a very deep significance transcending purely decorative values. Hindu artists use colour on the deities and their dresses signifying their qualities. Proper use of colours creates an environment which should keep a person cheerful. Some of the main colours used in religious ceremonies are red, yellow (turmeric), green from leaves, white from wheat flour etc.

Red – In Hindu religion, red is of utmost significance and the colour most frequently used for auspicious occasions like marriages, birth of a child, festivals etc. A red mark is put on the forehead during ceremonies and important occasions. As a sign of their marital status, women put red powder in their hair parting. They also wear a red sari during their wedding ceremony. Red powder is usually thrown on statues of deities and phallic symbols during prayers. It is also the colour of shakti (prowess). Deities who are charitable, brave, protective and who have the capacity to destroy evil are clothed in red. On the death of a woman, her body is wrapped in a red cloth for the cremation. Even the body of a widow is wrapped in red coloured cloth, the only difference being that the cloth wrapped round her is not embroidered or decorated.

Saffron – It represents fire and as impurities are burnt by fire, this colour symbolises purity. It also represents religious abstinence. It is the colour of holy men and ascetics who have renounced the world. Wearing the colour symbolises the quest for light. It is the battle colour of the Rajputs, the warrior caste.

Green – Symbolising peace and happiness, it stabilises the mind. The colour is cool to the eyes and represents nature.

Yellow – This is the colour of knowledge and learning. It symbolises happiness, peace, meditation, competence and mental development. It is the colour of spring and activates the mind. Lord Vishnu's dress is yellow symbolising his representation of knowledge. Lord Krishna and Ganesha also wear yellow dresses.

White – It is a mixture of seven different colours and hence it symbolises a little bit of the quality of each. It represents purity, cleanliness, peace and knowledge. The goddess of knowledge, Saraswati is always shown as wearing a white dress, sitting on a white lotus. The other prominent deities would also have a touch of white on their dress. A Hindu widow in mourning is clothed in white.

Blue – The Creator has given the maximum of blue to nature, i.e., the sky, the oceans, the rivers and lakes. The deity who has the qualities of bravery, manliness, determination, the ability to deal with difficult situations, of stable mind and depth of character is represented as blue coloured. Lord Rama and Krishna spent their life protecting humanity and destroying evil, hence they are coloured blue.

THE HOLY COW

The cow is sacred to the Hindus, a fact that puzzles the foreigner who finds numerous animals wandering the streets of the towns and cities, muzzling at fruit and vegetable stalls and sometimes obstructing traffic. The sacredness of the cow is a central and crucial element in Hindu belief. The cow is supposed to be the living symbol of Mother Earth. For the early migrants, the cow was an indispensable member of the family. As agriculture was the occupation of the migrants, the cow provided them with milk and its byproducts and also necessities of life such as fuel, manure for the farm, etc. During this time the Aryans prayed to their numerous gods through 'yagna' (from 'yaj', to worship). This was initially a simple way of private worship but became public in character and consisted of invoking the fire-god, Agni, by ritually kindling sacred wood on an altar, and keeping the fire alive by constantly feeding it with melted butter. It was through the instrumentality of Agni (fire) that the offering of milk-pudding and a drink of milk, curds and honey (madhupeya) was conveyed to one's chosen gods. Thus, the cow supplied the major requirements of the yagna and this association soon made it sacred.

Later, animal sacrifices waned as gradually the Hindus veered towards vegetarianism due to the influence of early Jainism and Buddhism, specially on the Brahmins and Vaishyas. Gradually, the cow came to be known as 'Gaumata'(cow, the Mother) and 'Aditi' (mother of gods). The rise of Vaishnavism amongst the prosperous middle and lower castes (expressed in the figure of the cowherd god Krishna) helped consolidate the importance and the religious glorification of the cow. Some of the other factors which resulted in its sanctity were its figurative usage in Vedic literature which later was taken literally; prohibitions against killing a Brahmin's (priest's) cow, and lastly, the symbol of cow protection as an affirmation of religious solidarity against Muslim invaders.

DHARMA

Dharma means social and moral order, law, duty, right, virtue and so on. It means righteousness or good ethical practice according to the

prescriptions passed down from one generation to the next. Dharma designates the traditional established order, which includes all duties—individual, social and religious. Dharma is threatened and endangered by three great moral pitfalls—lust, covetousness and anger (kama, lobha and krodha). Besides the general prescriptions contained in Dharma, every man has his own (self) Dharma (svadharma), which is determined by his place in the social structure. The correct working out of one's own Dharma, above all other obligations, is one of the primary themes of the Bhagavad Gita.

THE FOUR STAGES OF LIFE

A Hindu's life in the ancient times was divided into four stages—Brahmacharya (celibacy), Grahasthya (householdership), Vanaprastha and Sanyas. This lifestyle, with centuries of Muslim and British influence, has more or less died out and not practised any more. Short notes are given on each stage as they used to be practised in the ancient times

Brahmacharya (Celibacy)—This was the first stage (up to the age of twenty-five) when the student, after the thread ceremony, left his home and joined the 'gurukula' (school), normally a simple group of huts set inside a forest or a lonely place away from habitation. Here the teacher or guru lived with his family and students, who must, irrespective of social status, look after the guru like one's father and perform all menial chores around the school. Here they were taught the Gayatri mantra, yoga, the study of the scriptures, the arts and sciences, and a life of simplicity and Spartan self-discipline. The students were exhorted to speak the truth, to work without forgetting Dharma, to serve the elders, to regard one's parents, teacher and guest as divine beings.

Grahasthya (Householdership)—After finishing his education, the student returned home to marry and set up a household. Marriage was not contractual and was a sacred step in one's spiritual growth. The wife was the ardhangini or the other half of her husband. No religious ritual could be performed by a man without his wife's participation therein. The householder was to practice right conduct, earn material wealth, permit himself a life of love and passion with his life partner and attain salvation by following the rules of conduct. The second stage was considered the most important of the four. The householder was expected to earn a living with integrity and to give away one-tenth of what he earned to charity. He was expected to give happiness and joy to his wife by providing her with a good home. It was obligatory for him to look after his children, educate and marry them. Charity and hospitality were essential. Fulfilling social and spiritual obligations of life, with its trials and tribulations and without deviation from Dharma, enables a person to evolve into a superior human being.

Vanaprastha—The third stage comes when one's children are settled and can look after themselves. It is time for the middle-aged couple to become vanaprasthas, or those who retire. In modern parlance this means that the time has come for one to detach oneself from worldly desires and attachments and retire to the sylvan peace of contemplation, meditation and spiritual pursuits. They may live amongst their family but remain unattached from within, like a lotus which is in water yet out of it.

Sanyas—This used to be the fourth stage. One who took to sanyas gave up all wants, had no needs, would not accept money and renounced the world. He used to live on alms and the fruits of trees in the forest and spent his time in meditation. He was jivanmukta or one liberated from ordinary life.

FUNERAL RITES

Amongst orthodox Hindus, there are many variations of the funeral rites, depending on region and social stratum. A religious–minded person approaching death would wish to pass his last moments on earth in the holy city of Varanasi, on the banks of the sacred Ganga river, as it is said that a person dying there will be delivered from all sins. For an ordinary Hindu funeral the dead body is bathed with Ganga water, perfumed, wrapped in white cloth (red for women) and carried to the cremation site on a wooden stretcher-like structure, to the accompaniment of the chanting of the words 'Ram Nam Satya Hai' (Rama is Truth). In the case of some kings, feudal lords and sadhus, the body is taken out on the 'stretcher' in a sitting posture.

The nearest relation, normally the eldest son, lights the funeral pyre. This is important as whoever lights the pyre is considered the legal heir. Vedic verses are chanted during the cremation by the priest and the next day the ashes are collected and taken to Haridwar, the headwaters of the Ganga, and immersed in the holy water there. In the days following the cremation, a mourning period of approximately twelve days is observed, during which time the relatives and visitors have to sit on the floor.

Every year certain days are set aside during which the family members must remember their dead ancestors and relatives and pray for the peace of their souls. This period is called shraadh.

GURU

Guru is a spiritual guide and teacher who leads a disciple or pupil (sisya or chela) onto the spiritual path, directing him to Final realisation. At the proper point, the guru will bestow initiation on his disciple and give him the sacred saying (mantra) that will guide him for the rest of his life.

According to the tantrics, the human guru is but a manifestation on the phenomenal plane of the Supreme Guru. Traditionally, the guru incarnates the highest value anyone may look for in a human being. Ideally, the disciple lives for twelve years with his guru learning the Way of Life. A true guru never advertises nor does he look for disciples. The true guru exists, with his disciples, in the depths of silence, relying on voluntary contributions for sustenance. One must seek out his guru who will test his would-be disciple severely, even to the point of rejecting him. One retains his guru for life. On acceptance, at the beginning of the relationship, the guru often, if not invariably, demolishes the disciple's ego in order to rebuild.

THE HINDU MARRIAGE

The majority of Hindu marriages are arranged by the parents though this is changing now, specially in the cosmopolitan cities. It is considered highly improper for a young man or woman to take the initiative for his or her marriage. With the spread of education nowadays the boy and the girl are given a chance to see each other, unlike the old days when the newly weds saw each other only after the marriage.

The initiative for the proposal must always come from the girl's side, usually through an intermediary. In olden days, the intermediary was generally a priest or a barber, but, nowadays it is usually a common friend of both the families. Once the negotiations begin, the priest takes over and the horoscopes are matched. A horoscope that does not match is said to lead to an unharmonious marriage.

A betrothal ceremony (tilak) is held which is more or less the solemnisation of the forthcoming marriage contract. For this ceremony, usually, only close friends and relatives are invited. For the main ceremony the priests fix the month, the day and the exact time of the ceremony after taking into consideration the influence of the planets. On the lucky day, the boy is taken in a procession to the bride's house, sitting on a horse, and led by a group of musicians and male members of the family and friends. Ladies are not usually allowed to take part in the procession in some communities. All ceremonies take place in the bride's house and she normally doesn't set out of her house during the marriage period.

For the actual ceremony, the boy, with some close friends, enters the room where the ceremony is to take place while the rest of the party are entertained lavishly in a separate hall. The groom is usually welcomed at the entrance of the bride's house. This dwara-puja (door-prayers) is an important part of the ceremony and is usually done by putting a tilak on the forehead and the waving of lighted lamps in front of the groom.

The actual ceremony takes a long time and usually starts in the evening and goes on past midnight. The marriage hall is decorated with flowers and colours of all kinds. The bride and the groom, dressed in

all their finery, sit cross-legged side by side in front of the sacred fire, with the priest sitting on one side chanting the sacred verses and the parents of the girl on the other side.

Before the ceremony begins, Lord Ganesha, the remover of obstacles is worshipped. The bride's face is usually veiled. One end of a piece of consecrated cloth is tied to the boy's dress and the other end to the bride's. Then the bride's father gives the hand of his daughter in that of the bridegroom to the chanting of sacred prayers. The bride and the groom then clasp each other's hands, usually with crushed leaves of the mehendi plant put in between. The hands are then covered with a piece of cloth and a thread wrapped around. During the ceremony the bride and the groom are asked to throw rice, clarified butter, etc., into the fire at definite stages of the proceedings. The role of the bride and the groom is passive though they do repeat certain prayers after the priest.

The marriage is solemnised irrevocably when the bride and the groom together take seven rounds of the sacred fire, representing the god Agni, the most truthful and straight-dealing of the gods. The farewell ceremony is held the next day when the girl is sent off to her husband's house to start a new life. Formerly marriages used to take more than a week but nowadays they take a couple of days.

There are many variations of the above ceremonies depending on the community, region and caste.

INCARNATION (AVATARA)

All incarnation is a manifestation of God on earth. Lord Krishna in the Gita states: "whenever righteousness declines and unrighteousness prevails, I manifest myself. For the protection of the righteous and the destruction of the wicked, and for the establishment of religion, I come into being from age to age". Thus God took human form again and again to destroy evil. This doctrine reached its fullest development during the Puranic period (A.D. 300-1200).

The avataras or incarnations reconciled the unity of the divine with the multiplicity of local divinities, thus absorbing tribal, racial and community gods. Of the many avataras, those of Vishnu are the most popular, the best known being Rama and Krishna. The avataras of the epics are intermediaries between man and the divine. God manifests himself in forms that can be appreciated by even the most unsophisticated.

Avataras are countless, for besides the popularly known figures, any saint or spiritual teacher can be said to be an avatara to some degree, being at least in part, if not fully, an embodiment of the divine.

KARMA

One of the basic beliefs of Hinduism is the law of Karma or Action. It basically means that every good thought, word or deed begets a similar reaction which affects our next lives, and every unkind thought or evil deed comes back to harm us in this life or the next. There are three stages of Karma:

Prarabdha Karma—According to this, the body or tenement the soul chooses to be born in is not under human control and depends on the sum-total of favourable and unfavourable acts performed in a previous life. So also the time of death. If your time on earth is not over, you cannot die no matter what happens, but when your time comes nothing can save you.

Samchita Karma—This is the accumulated Karma of previous births which gives us our characteristics, aptitudes, etc. This is reversible and an evil man can take a turn for the better, get rid of evil thoughts and desires while a good man can fall on evil ways.

Agami Karma—This Karma consists of actions in our present life which determine our future in this life as well as in the next.

The best or ideal Karma is the one which is performed as a point of duty towards God or mankind without seeking any rewards (**Nishkama Karma**).

LOTUS FLOWER

The lotus (padma) is born in water and unfolds itself into a beautiful flower. Hence it is taken as the symbol of the universe coming out of the Sun. It rises from the navel of Vishnu, and is the seat of Brahma,

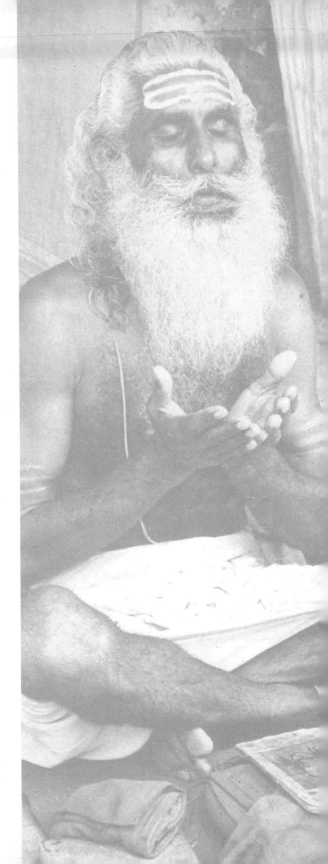

the Creator, and therefore the sacredness associated with it. It symbolises self creation. Psychic centres (*see* Chakra) in the body associated with the rising of the Kundalini power are pictured like lotuses. The padma or lotus pedestal is indicative of divinity and a number of deities are shown standing or sitting on it.

MAHABHARATA

The epic Mahabharata depicts Indo-Aryan society at the zenith of its glory and is a work of great antiquity. In its present form, it is said to have been compiled around the A.D. fourth century. The Mahabharata is supposed to have one hundred thousand verses in Sanskrit language, composed by the sage Veda Vyas.

The story centres upon two brothers, Dhritarashtra and Pandu. Dhritarashtra was blind, therefore unfit to rule, but was the regent for Pandu's sons (the Pandavas) after his death. Duryodhana, the eldest of Dhritarashtra's hundred sons (the Kauravas) was jealous and could not understand how the Pandavas were to be the heirs when his father was the elder brother. Court intrigues started and the Pandavas had to go into exile where they formed secret alliances with many powerful kings including Krishna, Vishnu's incarnation and the king of Dwaraka. When they felt strong enough, they demanded their kingdom back. Duryodhana wanted to wage war but the court elders prevailed upon Dhritarashtra to divide the kingdom equally between the two groups. The Kauravas got Hastinapur as their capital and the Pandavas got Indraprastha (present greater Delhi). The Kauravas again became jealous and there were many petty quarrels culminating in the famous dice game in which the Pandavas lost everything, including their wife Draupadi. The Pandavas also had to bear the shame of the Kauravas wanting their wife to be stripped in public. They had to go into exile for twelve years during which there were many unsuccessful attempts to kill them. After the term of exile was over, the Pandava brothers demanded their kingdom back and on the refusal of the Kauravas, a full-scale war was fought for eighteen days on the fields of Kurukshetra (near Delhi). In the battle thousands of combatants died, the only survivors being the Pandavas. They got disillusioned with all the bloodshed that had taken place and, after installing their grandson Parikshit on the throne, started on a long and perilous journey towards the heaven of god Indra, beyond the great Himalayas.

MANDALA

The word means circle and thus mandala is a complex diagram in circular form employed for the focusing of cosmic and psychic energies. It may be as small as a drawing or as large as a temple enclosure. The yantra is a form of mandala different only in that the former embodies but a single deity while the latter may enclose an infinite number. The mandala is an image of the universe, a receptacle for the gods. As sacred space, it is a form of paradise, purified of demons. Through the mandalas, the participants seek protection from the malignant forces of nature.

The mandala diagrams, when awakened and made operative by incantation and ritual gesture, could create, enclose, protect and destroy energy. The mandala diagram had gateways which were guarded by mantras (prayers). A small mandala provides the yogi with an image of the world into which he enters psychically.

MANTRA

It is a properly repeated hymn or formula used in ritual worship and meditation as an instrument for evoking the presence of a particular divinity; first uttered by an inspired seer (rishi) and transmitted orally from master to disciple in a carefully controlled manner. A mantra may be composed of but a single sound (om), or several syllables. Each deity is represented by its own mantra. It is only by the correct enunciation of the correct mantra that the deity will descend to enter the body of its image, or will respond to a devotee. A mantra has great potency and represents the Supreme Being Himself in the guise of sound. The disciple must keep his mantra secret and say it silently as part of his regular worship. Other mantras are openly known and commonly said, e. g. the Gayatri Mantra, which forms part of the morning ritual.

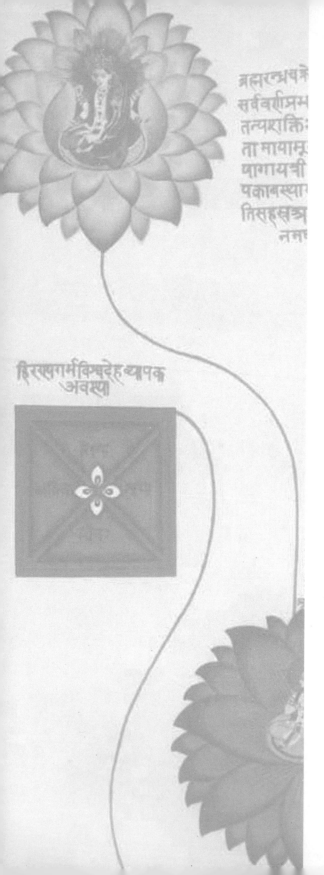

MOKSHA

Moksha means liberation from the stream-current of life, from the chain of Karma. Moksha is not a negative state but one of completeness, of fullness, of being free from the bondage of Karma, and thus from the endless round of birth, death and rebirth, leading to Nirvana, the final freedom expressed in unity in the Supreme. Moksha is attained through three ways or paths—knowledge, devotion and ritual works (Karma). Some may attain Moksha at death, but the goal is to achieve it well in advance, as certain yogis and the true gurus do. A guru in the fullest sense of the word should be 'jivan-mukta', i.e., one who has attained liberation before death. Thus, Moksha is the highest aim of human existence.

NAMASKAR

Namaskar is the most popular form of greeting in India. It is a general salutation and is used as a welcome as well as a farewell. Namaskar also means 'I bow to thee'. The palms are placed together and raised to touch the forehead, the site of the Third Eye. Together, the hands symbolise the One Mind, or the self meeting the Self, the right hand representing the holy, or higher nature, and the left, the worldly, or lower nature. Another term used for this greeting is namaste. Namaste may have originated in the ancient times as a showing of hands to prove that no arms were being carried.

NIRVANA

Nirvana is the union with the Supreme (Brahman), through moksha, i.e., release from the cycle of birth and death and the pain, sorrow, and suffering of the human condition. Nirvana is the immediate experience of the ego-less self with the blissful Brahman. The Bhagavad-Gita has one of the clearest expositions of Nirvana, calling it Brahma-nirvana, i.e., union with Brahman, or extinction (of the ego) in Him. The Gita's method is by the practice of yoga (joy, peace, vision all turning inward), through which one can 'come to Brahman and know nirvana'. The Jains have somewhat similar ideas expressed in their own terms.

RAMAYANA

Written by the sage Valmiki, The Ramayana is a smaller work than the Mahabharata, having about 24,000 couplets.

The fortunes of Rama, the seventh incarnation of Vishnu, form the main theme of the epic. The prince who was virtuous, brave and kind was the eldest son of king Dasharatha who, as he grew old, decided to crown Rama as king and then retire. On the eve of the coronation, Kaikeye, the youngest wife of Dasharatha, through manipulation extracted a promise from him to get her son Bharata installed as the king and exile Rama, his wife Sita, and half-brother Lakshman to the jungles of the Deccan.

Bharata, who was away when this was happening, was full of remorse and followed Rama to the jungles and offered his kingdom back to him. This meeting of the brothers is described with much pathos and tenderness. But Rama would not cause the promise given by his father to be broken and sent his brother back to rule as his regent.

From this point the real saga begins. Ravana, the demon king of Lanka (Ceylon) came to hear about the beauty of Sita and abducted her, carrying her away in his aerial chariot, Pushpak. Rama and Lakshmana were out at that time and on returning, set out on a search for Sita. After long wanderings in the forests they found out her whereabouts with the help of wild bears and monkey tribes that inhabited the hills. Under Rama's leadership, an army of monkeys was raised who built a bridge across the gulf between the mainland and Lanka, and stormed Lanka. After many bloody battles, the ten-headed Ravana was killed and Sita reclaimed. After the exile Rama returned to Ayodhya with many of the monkey chiefs. Of them, Hanuman was considered the most loyal and brave and is worshipped at present by the Hindus as a god.

RUDRAKSHA BEADS

The Rudraksha is one of the most commonly used beads amongst the Hindus. The tree on which it grows belongs to the species of *Elaeocarpus Ganitrus* found in the Himalayas. The seed of the fruit of this tree is used as a bead and is classified into four categories according to their shape and sizes. They are:

Rudraksha—This is round and large in size and most commonly used for prayers, medicines and for making garlands.

Bhadraksha—This one is smaller in size and round. It is less beneficial than Rudraksha.

Indraksha—This is shaped like a groundnut and is oval.

Sahastraksha. It is shaped like Indraksha, only it is slightly flat in shape.

The bead is classified on the basis of the number of lines or mouths (mukhas) running from top to bottom. The number of mouths can vary from one to fourteen. The five-mouthed (pancha mukha) beads are the most common while those having one to four and six to fourteen are the most rare, fetching the highest price.

A single faced bead is the rarest and the owner will be free from the cycle of births and rebirths. The double faced one is sacred to Shiva and his shakti, the three-faced one to the trinity and the three shaktis. The four-faced one is associated with Brahma and the four Vedas. The five-faced one is to Shiva and the six faced one to Kartikeya. On wearing the seven-faced bead the goddess Mahalakshmi is happy. The eight-faced one is to Ganesha and the wearer is always victorious. The nine-faced bead represents the nine shaktis (Durga). The ten-faced one represents the ten directions and is specially useful. The eleven faced one represents Rudra, the twelve faced one, the Sun, and the thirteen faced one removes all evil. The fourteen-faced one represents fourteen manifestations and also destroys all evil.

The seeds are generally of four colours. The most highly prized are the white, the reddish, the golden and the dark. The first and the

third varieties are rare. Their superiority is not on the basis of rarity but on the four 'varanas', white being suggestive of Brahmin, red of Kshatriya, gold of Vaisya and the dark of the Sudra.

Legend has it that the Rudraksha seed was created from the tears of Rudra, the fierce form of Shiva, thus endowing it with medicinal, occult and spiritual powers. Each of the fourteen types of beads has a governing deity and specific properties. The smaller the size of the bead, the greater its efficacy. The bead that has a natural opening to allow the string to pass is considered the most sacred.

Rituals and observances are prescribed along with the wearing of this bead for getting the desired results. Its contact with the body is essential to derive its magical powers. It may be worn singly on a white thread or in a garland. A genuine Rudraksha bead is supposed to be beneficial to a person for good health and well-being.

The smaller beads are used in rosaries, normally of twenty-seven, fifty-four or one hundred and eight beads and are considered very effective in meditation while chanting the prayers.

Apart from the general classification, unusual shaped beads are highly valued by devout Hindus. The test of a genuine Rudraksha is that it will sink to the bottom if put in a glass of water. The major trade of this bead is concentrated in the holy cities of India, like Varanasi and Haridwar.

SACRED MOUNTAINS

Mountains, which occupy an important place in Hindu mythology, are a symbol of strength when certain gods in their fury grow to resemble mountains, and of oppressive weight when they are torn up and used as missiles by gods or demons. The most important of these are of course the Himalayas, on the summits of which are the heavens.

Mountains, specially the Himalayas, were also important as it was amongst them that the holy men, the yogis and the sadhus lived doing meditation. It was here that the important ashramas of the gurus were located and many are still functioning. A person going on a trek in the Himalayas can easily find yogis doing meditation in caves amongst the high snow-capped peaks.

Some of the important mountains are:

Meru, which bears on its summit Brahma's heaven, and acts as a pivot for the three worlds around which the heavenly bodies revolve.

Himavan, which took the form of a man when the gods wished Sati to be reborn, and became the father of first the Ganga, and then of Parvati.

Mandara, which is a revered mountain in the Himalayas and was thought to be the only one mighty enough to serve as a pole in the churning of the milk ocean. It became the home of Durga.

Mount Kailash, the home of Shiva, which became involved in a dispute between Indra and Kartikeya as to their relative powers and to settle the dispute they agreed to race around it. Kartikeya won but became angry when Kailash gave the verdict in favour of Indra and hurled his lance at the mountain splitting it open, thus creating the Krauncha pass.

Some other holy mountains are **Parijat, Malyagiri, Mahendrachal, Chitrakoot, Goverdhan** (Mathura), **Kamagiri** (Assam), **Shaktiman** (Madhya Pradesh) and **Raiwatgiri** (Gujarat).

SACRED PLACES

For the Hindus, to visit the holy places is an act of great religious merit. Throughout India there are centres of pilgrimage, some of them very holy, others less so. Great emphasis is laid on visiting the holy places (yatra) once in a life-time for the attainment of salvation. Four of the holy places have been established by Adi Shankaracharya (a saint) and it signifies a farsightedness of vision towards national integration as they are situated at the four corners of India, making devotees criss-cross the country.

Benares is the most sacred among the holy places. Also known as Varanasi and Kashi, it is the city of Shiva, having over two thousand temples and over half a million idols, most of them dedicated to Shiva and his family. It is situated on the banks of the holy river Ganga.

Mathura, on the banks of the Jamuna, near Agra, is the birth place of Krishna. The atmosphere of Mathura is in direct contrast to that of Benares. Mathura represents the religion of the living, while Benares emphasises the permanence of death.

Dwaraka in Gujarat is another important shrine. It was the capital of Krishna's kingdom and has some very important temples devoted to him. The city is located on the Western coast of India.

Puri in Orissa has the Jagannath temple which attracts pilgrims from all over India. It has an idol considered to be a manifestation of Krishna. The temple, containing idols of Balarama and Subhadra (sister of Krishna), is on the Eastern corner of India.

Rameswaram, from where Rama is said to have launched his attack on Lanka, is in the extreme south of India. Rama is said to have installed a Shiva lingam here; hence the place is sacred to both Shaivas (Shiva worshippers) and Vaishnavas (Vishnu worshippers).

Gaya on the Ganges, once a stronghold of the Buddhists, is for the Hindus connected with the death ceremonies of ancestors for which they visit the place. After the rituals are performed at Gaya the soul of the dead is supposed to attain salvation.

Ujjain. It is called the navel of earth. It has the famous temples of Ganesha and Kal-Bhairav. During the time of Vikramaditya it used to be the capital of India. Two parts of the Skanda-Purana were said to have been written here.

Haridwar. It is another very important holy city of India. It is at the foothills of the Himalayas and is the place where the Ganga enters the plains. It is also called the 'gateway of the Ganga'.

Other important holy places are; **Ayodhya** (Rama's capital), **Kanchi** (Conjeevaram), **Kedarnath, Somnath, Amarnath** and **Kamakhya.**

SACRED RIVERS

In India rivers are given a divine status. The civilisation of India was nurtured in the river basin of the Ganga and the Jamuna which has been the heart of ancient India. The two rivers have, therefore, been worshipped since ancient times. The **Ganga** has been known for its purity and divinity and the Hindus believe that a bath in her waters cleanses one of all sins. The river **Jamuna** is known for her devotion. The river **Saraswati** was worshipped in ancient times when the Aryans lived in Punjab. The Saraswati changed its course in later ages and gradually disappeared in the deserts of Rajasthan. Apart from these three, the other rivers considered sacred are the **Godavari, Narmada, Sindhu** (Indus) and **Kaveri** (Cauvery). Some other sacred rivers are **Saryu, Gomti, Gandaki, Sabarmati, Tarnsa, Chandarbhaga, Shipra** and **Kratmala.**

Around A.D. fourth century, architects began to carve figures of Ganga and Jamuna, in human form, on the two sides of the temple door symbolising purity (Ganga) and devotion (Jamuna). This was to emphasise that only the pure and devoted could enter the temples. At a later period it became a common practice to represent the two river goddesses on the two sides of the shrine door in both North and South India.

SACRED TREES AND PLANTS

For Hindus, everything in the universe is sacred and whatever grows, is more so. In Hinduism, animistic beliefs find a place side by side with the highest philosophical and religious speculation, and are often expressed mystically and esoterically. The tree deity has been found in the stamp seals of the Indus Valley civilisation.

Sacred groves, homes of mother goddesses, abound and some types of trees have attained great importance in Hinduism. Plants such as the tulsi, a type of basil, are equally important.

The spirits that inhabit trees are the yakshas, feminine deities; male figures never appear in such a connection. Veneration of the tree is a form of Shaktism, the cult of the Great Mother.

A yaksha is propitiated with offerings such as food, bits of cloth tied to the branches and red-smeared stones put at the base of the tree. Some trees, like the tulsi, are worshipped daily, some every month, while some others are worshipped only during specific festivals.

Some of the important trees and plants are described below.

Pipal *(Ficus religiosa)* is one of the foremost trees in Hinduism and Buddhism. It is also known as the bodhi tree because Gautama Buddha attained enlightenment under it. The tree is the object of universal worship throughout India. It is sacred to Vishnu. It is a very large tree with high raised roots which descend to the ground from the branches like additional trunks.

Other important trees sacred to Vishnu are the **Banyan** or Indian Fig tree *(Ficus Indica)*, **Chandra-mallika** *(Chrysanthemum indicum)*, **Naga Keshara** *(Mesuaferrea)*, etc. Trees sacred to Shiva are the famous **Ashoka** *(Saraca Indica)* with pointed leaves, **Kesara** *(Mimusops Elengi)*, **Champaka** *(Michela Champaca)*, and **Vata** amongst others.

Lakshmi has **Kamala** *(Nelumbium speciosum)* while Parvati has **Sri-phala** *(Aegle Marnielos)* as their representatives.

The **Kaila** or plantain is sacred to one of the forms of Kali. It is commonly used in marriages and during festivals, a decorative doorway is made out of it, leading to the temple or the room where the prayers are to be held.

Tulsi *(Ocynum sanctum)* is a sacred plant of the basil family. Tulsi was one of Vishnu's paramours. Out of jealousy his wife Lakshmi turned her into a plant, and the god became the salagrama stone to keep her company. In some versions of the story, Tulsi and Lakshmi are the same. The plant is about three feet in height. Everyday the ground near it is covered with a layer of cowdung and at night a lamp is lit near it. It is a common custom to place a sprig of tulsi near the head of a dying person. The aromatic leaves are taken as a digestive after meals.

In addition to the above, the **Kusha Grass** *(Poa cynosuroides)* and **Durva Grass** *(Agrostis linearis)* are also considered very sacred.

The kusha has the quality of warding off evil. In all rituals, kusha is a must in some form or other. Durva is supposed to be very auspicious and is offered to Ganesha.

SADHUS

The Sadhu (also known as yogi and sanyasi), is a Hindu ascetic who has renounced caste, social position, money and authority, and occupies a special place in Hindu society. As one who seeks the Universal Soul in order to be absorbed in it, the Sadhu is set apart from the orthodox priesthood as renunciation is considered superior to the rituals of the priests.

The concept of the Sadhu traces its origin to the earliest images of Shiva himself, with his matted hair and the body covered with ash. A Sadhu does not have any caste and is free to attach himself to any strata of the social structure. The Sadhu is credited with much of the development of Indian culture, art, architecture, music, poetry and literature, influencing and forming the very world he has abandoned with his endless travels from one sacred site to another, singing songs and reciting poetry and carrying icons, paintings and other sanctified objects.

The Sadhu usually wears, on his forehead, the three lines of the god's trident drawn in ash or sandalwood paste which may be vertical or horizontal. Endless variations of these sectarian marks, depending on the sect, are possible. They may decorate their bodies with various lines and markings, cover the entire torso with ash, carry a metal trident and wear rosaries. The hair and the beard are uncut and matted.

Shaivite Sadhus are followers of Shiva and are divided into various sects. The Dasanami (monks with ten names) sect has about ten branches scattered all over India. They each have an armed militant branch called the Nagas. They follow Tantrism and Shaktism, eat meat, take stimulants and are often criticised for their erotic practices. The

Gorakhnathis wear large earrings. The **Aghori Yogis** are notorious for their rites involving the dead. The **Lingayats** centre their worship on the linga as the symbol of Shiva.

Vaishnavite Sadhus are devoted to Vishnu and are a later development than the Shaivite. Commonly called Vairagi (detached ones), they are members of various schools of Bhakti (devotion). They do not emphasise the ascetic extremes of the Shaivites. Their common identifying mark is a white V drawn on the forehead, with an added line in either white or red in the centre. They normally wear white and carry beads of the tulsi (sacred basil). Unlike the common Hindu who is cremated, the Sadhu is buried, usually in the sitting position. The burial site normally becomes a place of worship.

SALAGRAMA STONE

The Salagrama is a small stone, actually an ammonite, a fossil genus of marine cephalophod, and is considered by Brahmins to be a natural representation of Vishnu. It plays an important role in the worship of a Brahmin, who is considered a living, earthly form of the deity. The salagrama is mentioned in the Atharva Veda where it is written that any Brahmin's house that does not contain the salagrama is to be considered as impure as a cemetery.

Salagramas are to be found in the Gundak river in Nepal. They are black or dark coloured, round or oval in shape, striated, umbilicated and ornamented with natural tree like markings. The most sought after are the ones that are perforated in one or more places by worms. The curves of the striations signify the various forms of Vishnu. A black Salagrama with a replica of the discus in it is capable of bestowing great happiness, health, wealth and children. A half green Salagrama will drive away all sins and one which has the shape of the umbrella on it will make the possessor a monarch. The worship of Salagrama does not call for elaborate prayer ceremonies. Its very presence assures happiness.

The reason for its sacredness is that once Shani called on Vishnu, who had transformed himself into a mountain. This angered Shani who became a worm (Vajrakita) and afflicted him for twelve years. At the

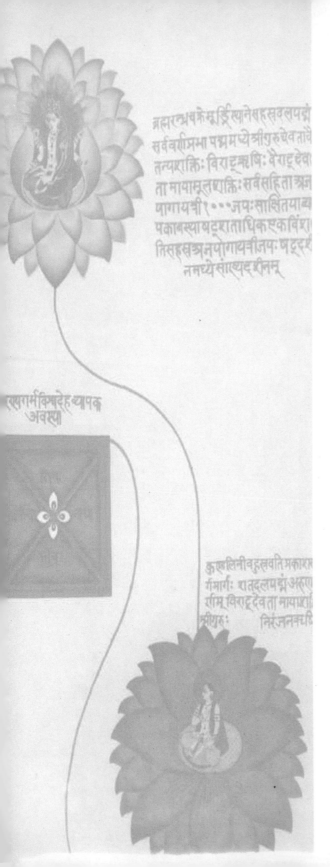

expiration of the time, Vishnu regained his original shape and ordered that henceforth the stones of this mountain will be worshipped as a representation of himself.

The salagrama is kept in the home, wrapped in a cloth, frequently bathed and perfumed and sometimes having water dripping on it. Though the stone is Vishnu in its visual form, it is also a lingam, the Shiva phallus, and a type of the Cosmic Egg.

SECTS AND SECTARIAN MARKS

The various sects and the sub-sects of the Hindus are distinguished by the symbols of the deities they worship. These are marked on their foreheads, arms and chests. The forehead marks are, of course, the most prominent but nowadays only the orthodox Hindus wear them. Some put them on only during festivals or prayers.

Some of the common sects are:

a) The Saivas (Shaivites) who worship Shiva and Parvati jointly.

b) The Vaishnavites who worship Vishnu.

c) The Suras, who worship Surya (Sun).

The Saivas may be further subdivided into Saiva proper who worship the linga-yoni symbol; the Lingaits who worship Shiva in his linga or phallic form; the Saktas who worship the yoni or the female form of Shiva -'shakti', i.e., female energy (they may worship the female energy of Krishna or Rama also) and the Ganapatis who worship Ganesha, son of Shiva.

The other major sect, the Vaishnavas, may be subdivided into two. The first, the Gokulas, worship Vishnu as Krishna, with or without his consort Radha. There are some who worship Radha only. The second, Ramanuj, worship Rama alone or with Sita, his consort, while there are some who worship Sita alone.

The Vaishnavas are distinguished by perpendicular lines on the forehead, with or without a dot or circlet between them, or by a chakra or discus, or a triangle, shield, cone, heart-shape or any similar form having its apex pointed downward, since Vishnu is water, the property of which is to descend (B in the diagram).

The Saivas are distinguished by two or more horizontal lines, with or without a dot below or above them, or on the middle line with or without the oval, or half-oval, typical of his third eye bisecting the lines; also by a triangle, or any pointed or arched object having its apex or convex end upward, since Shiva is fire—the property of which is to ascend. The crescent moon and the trident (trisul) also indicate a votary of Shiva (C in the diagram).

A. Marks of followers of Brahma and the Trinity

B. Marks of followers of Vishnu

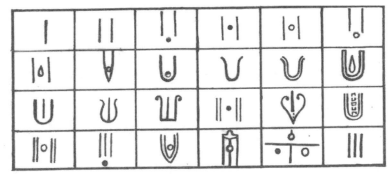

C. Marks of followers of Shiva

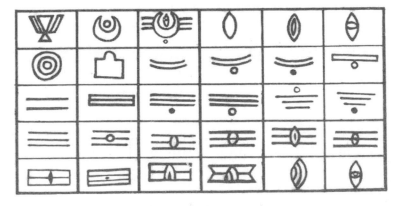

101

Images of Ganesha and Kartikeya bear the marks of Shiva while those of Indra, Agni, Chandra, Krishna, Rama, Buddha and Hanuman bear the marks of Vishnu. Brahma, who is both water and fire, bears the sectarian marks of both Vishnu and Shiva (A in the diagram on the opposite page).

The dot is the mark of the Supreme Being and, with the lines of Vishnu or Shiva, indicates that the devotee claims that Vishnu or Shiva, as the case may be, is the supreme Godhead. The horizontal lines of the Saivas are white and the dot or circlet is red.

The sectarian marks are drawn in red, yellow, black, and ashen white and are made of ashes taken from the sacrificial fire, cowdung, turmeric, sandalwood, lime and an adhesive made from rice water.

SHIVA-LINGA

The Shiva-linga as a symbol of the creative power of Lord Shiva is the most widely venerated cult object in Saivism. The Shiva-linga is usually made of stone and has three parts. The base is a square with a octagonal or oval platform or pedestal in which is embedded a cylindrical, round topped stone.

A Shiva-linga may be movable (chal) or immovable (achal). The movable linga may be kept in a shrine in one's home and may be prepared temporarily with clay or dough and dispensed with after the worship. It may be made as a small pendant and worn on the body. The immovable lingas are those installed in temples and it is very common to have a linga in a temple without any image of Lord Shiva.

The lingas will always have an arrangement for water to drip on it continuously. During prayers it is bathed, bedecked with flowers and garlands, covered with oil and milk and offered rice and food. The linga may be shaped or natural elliptical stones picked up from riverbeds (bana-lingas).

The linga symbolises the divine act of creation. It represents the union of linga (phallic symbol) with the yoni (female organ) showing manifest nature, the universal energy.

SHRAADH

It is a system of offerings for deceased ancestors, based upon the Vedas. It is perhaps the strongest feature of Vedic Hinduism to have survived into the modern period. On the day of the death of a person, it is the eldest living son who serves as the sacrificer in the cremation rites and who conducts the ceremony so that the spirit of the deceased can join his or her ancestors. It is believed that without these ceremonies, the spirit can become a troublesome ghost. Ceremonies and rituals take place for eleven days culminating on the twelfth day when priests are fed and given presents, sometimes of great value.

In addition to these shraadhs linked to a specific death, other shraadhs for the ancestors may be held on the new-moon of each month or annually when the ancestors, represented by Brahmin (priest) surrogates are fed. Food is also given to crows, cows etc. Shraadh rituals performed on the banks of the sacred river at centres like Benares or Gaya are beneficial for the spirits of the ancestors.

STATUS OF WOMEN IN HINDU SOCIETY

The position of women in society is always an index of the greatness of its religion and culture. A woman has always been given a much higher status and position in Hinduism than in any other religion.

Women so inclined could avail themselves of the highest learning and there were many female seers and philosophers. In the ancient times Gargi, wife of Mandanamishra, was appointed as judge because of her superior erudition and spiritual attainments. Warrior queens, like Kaikeye, helped their husbands on the battlefields.

Women were not married till they were in their late teens, sometimes even later. They could choose their own husbands and inter-marriages were common. Polygamy existed in some societies but mostly amongst princes who contracted several marriages with daughters of neighbouring rulers for political reasons.

A woman was supposed to be the manifestation of Goddess/Shakti and the male (Shaktiman) was supposed to be incomplete without the female (Shakti) with him, whether he was a god or a human being. Each male deity of the Divine Trinity has his female counterpart; Saraswati (learning), Lakshmi (wealth) and Parvati (power). The rituals, especially auspicious ones, are incomplete when performed by a man without his wife co-participating. Dishonour to women was tantamount to dishonour of the Almighty. The wife or mother commanded more honour and reverence than husband or father.

With the onslaught of foreign invasions and the subsequent rigidity of the caste system, Hindu women lost their independence and became objects requiring male protection. In the process they lost the opportunities they earlier had of acquiring knowledge and learning.

Starting from the early nineteenth century, there arose a new upsurge of intellectual searching and re-evaluation of our ancient past with several reformers spreading the message of the need for purifying Hinduism of its excessive rites, rituals and orthodoxy and the heaping of inequalities on women. Some of the reformers of the time were Rammohun Roy, Ishwar Chandra Vidyasagar, Swami Vivekananda and Mahatma Gandhi.

Women in modern Indian society have full freedom and equality including the right of inheritance.

SWASTIKA

The word 'Swasti' means auspicious, benevolent, a good deed or good wishes. The Swastika is considered auspicious and is painted on the doors of houses in India to ward off evil spirits. Its origin goes back to the Vedic times (4500-2500 B.C.), maybe even earlier. Seals with the Swastika symbol have been found at excavation sites in Harappa which date back about two thousand years. The Swastika is in the form of a Greek cross with the ends of the arms bent at right angles. The right-handed Swastika moves

in the clockwise direction and the left-handed in the counter-clockwise direction. The latter is considered an evil omen and generally never used.

The Swastika is said to represent the Sun or Lord Vishnu. In the Puranas it has been described as the 'Sudarshana Chakra' or the wheel of Vishnu and also symbolises the constant changes in the universe. The Swastika has also been associated with the Sun (the arms representing the sun's rays) and also with Ganesha, the pathfinder whose image is often found at the crossroads.

In the 'Siddhanta Saar' the hub of the Swastika has been described as the navel of Vishnu and the four lines as the four faces and four arms of Brahma. The Swastika is considered as a tantric symbol and is drawn in various stylised forms. It is a tradition to pray to it during religious festivals and auspicious occasions. During Diwali, the festival of lights, and the financial year-end for Hindu businessmen, new account books are opened and decorated with the Swastika symbol and the words 'Shubh-Labh' (meaning 'Auspicious Profit') next to it. Prayers are also held so that the goddess of wealth, Lakshmi, will be benevolent.

TANTRA

Tantra is a form of yogic practice leading to divine ecstasy through certain rites that emphasise the erotic and the forbidden. Tantra is centred upon 'shakti', the divine female power worshipped by the sadhakas (male practitioners) through the 'shaktis' named after the goddesses who are her earthly incarnation in the tantric ceremony. While traditional Hindu spirituality emphasises abstinence from physical, emotional and tactile pleasures, as well as the negation of the mundane world, tantra cultivates and makes use of them.

In place of liberation through renunciation, tantra teaches liberation through bhoga (enjoyment). The core of Tantra is the feminine, generative, reproductive principle 'shakti', without which the world would not function.

TANTRA AND EROTIC SCULPTURE

To varying degrees, Tantra touched virtually all of Indian culture, especially art, architecture, and literature. Tantra found an expression in the sensual sculpture of the Indian temples, which envisions the coupling of the male and the female as union with the divine and the total release of the soul in the godhead. The erotic is but a means to the eternal Brahman.

Another theory for erotic sculpture around the temple walls is that it is also a test for the devotee to see whether he has purged his mind of all sensual and worldly thoughts before he enters the temple.

STRUCTURE OF A HINDU TEMPLE

The structure of a Hindu temple is the same all over India but there may be certain additions to its basic form depending on the regional influence or the wealth of the temple and sometimes the political influence. For example, the double images in the 'garbha griha' and the high protective wall in some South Indian temples were meant to protect against the Muslim invaders.

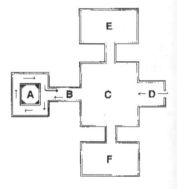

Hindu worship is not congregational in the Christian sense, and is mainly personal except on certain occasions. The structure of the temple is therefore based on the principle of having a small **garbha griha** (A in the diagram) where the image of the deity is installed. There is a passage for circumambulation of the garbha griha. This is the heart of the temple and the dome or spire is normally above the garbha griha, except in South Indian temples where the spire is generally at the entrance. Circumambulation after prayers is very necessary and the passage around the idol is an essential part of the structure of the temple.

There is a small passage called the **antrala** (vestibule) (B), which connects the garbha griha to the **mandapa** (C) or the pillared hall where the devotees gather for worship. The pillars normally have carvings of minor gods and goddesses, incidents from the life of the main deity and sometimes scenes from various epics.

In some temples, these carvings cover the exterior walls of the temples. The entrance porch is called the **ardha-mandapa** (D). In some of the larger temples, there are sometimes extra halls called the **maha mandapa** (E) **and kalyana mandapa** (F) used for holding large prayer meetings.

TILAK

The centre of the forehead between the eyebrows is the most important psychic location in the human body and its importance is stressed by putting a coloured mark at this spot. This central spot is where the sixth chakra (Ajna) is located. It is also called the third eye or the eye of wisdom. It is the aim of yogis and devout Hindus to 'open' this third eye by constant meditation. The 'opening' of the third eye means the unification of the conscious and subconscious minds, the point where all elements of duality merge into one universal entity.

This spot, therefore, is of tremendous importance and the putting of the coloured mark symbolises the quest for the 'opening' of the third eye. All rites and ceremonies of the Hindus begin with a vermilion mark (tilak) topped with a few grains of rice placed on this spot with the index finger or the thumb. The same custom is followed in welcoming or bidding farewell to guests or relations. One should not confuse the tilak with the bindi (shown in the illustration). One can see many ladies wearing what looks like a tilak, but, it is actually a bindi and is decorative. The bindi is mainly round but nowadays it comes in many attractive shapes and sizes.

The most common material used for making this mark is 'kumkum', a red powder which is a mixture of turmeric, alum, iodine, camphor, etc. Another popular material is sandalwood paste blended with musk. This has a strong cooling effect and is generally meant for those who have meditated for a long time.

Sacred ash from the sacrificial fire (yagna) or the funeral pyre is considered the best material for the tilak by yogis and sanyasis because they have renounced all their attachments to worldly life and ash symbolises this.

TRANSCENDENTAL MEDITATION

Transcendental meditation is a form of meditation (commonly called TM) derived from yogic principles (many of which have been discarded along the way). TM is not a religion, a philosophy or a way of life, but, a simple technique for expanding consciousness, offering access to a limited reservoir of energy and creative intelligence. TM has eliminated the five early stages of yoga to begin immediately with the sixth and aims at experiencing pure consciousness. The basic tool of TM is the 'mantra' given by the teacher at the first meeting and which is repeated and is the heart of the system. The 'mantra' is kept a secret and meditation is to be practised in a special room.

TM teachers and most students claim great success with the method and can cite numerous examples of individual overcoming anxieties, neuroses and psychosomatic conditions, in addition to gaining better health.

The followers of the orthodox path of Eastern disciplines charge that TM appeals to individuals who want 'instant enlightenment' without the preliminary basic training.

VEDAS

The word Veda means knowledge. There are four Vedas dating from the earliest period of known Indian scriptures; the Rig Veda, a collection of praises in the form of hymns; the Sama Veda, also a collection of hymns; the Yajur Veda, a collection of sacrificial formulas; and the Atharva Veda, a collection of charms and magic formulas. The texts were developed over a long period, possibly beginning before the Aryans arrived in India (B.C. 1700-1200). The texts were passed down orally, being handed on from one generation of priests to another, syllable perfect in intonation and rhythm, from memory and by rote. An error in recital led to punishment and penances; in effect, to hear a Vedic passage today is to hear the oral equivalent of a tape recording over three thousand years old. It was forbidden to write down the text, but about the A.D. fourteenth century, some parts of the Vedas were transcribed but the entire text is still a guarded province of scholarship.

YANTRA

Yantra is the visual form of mantra, a prayer. A tantric text states, 'Yantra has mantra as its soul. The deity is the soul of the mantra. The difference between mantra and deity is similar to that between a body and its soul'. Though two-dimensional, yantras are conceived of as having depth and full dimension. Yantras may be drawn or painted on any material, out of any substance. However, the human body is often called the best of all yantras by tantrics. There is no parallel for the term in English, but yantra may be summarised as a two-dimensional diagram where visualised energies are concentrated, or simply, a field of energy.

With its mantra, a yantra is a complex of stored imagery of sight and sound and psychic and mystical content. Many yantras seem to be nothing more than an interwoven complex of geometrical designs centred upon a point (bindu). Triangles, sign of the yoni, may predominate, enclosing the point. The whole may be enclosed by a square, signifying the cosmic dynamics and the four corners of the universe. Yantras are thus worshipped as containing the divine presence. The yantra is often confused with a mandala, but, the former is appropriate to a specific deity only, while the latter may enclose an infinite number of deities. It is an image of the universe, a receptacle of the gods.

There are innumerable yantras. Of them the one illustrated here is the most famous and is known as the Sri Chakra or Sri Yantra.

YOGA

The word 'yoga' means to yoke or unite and is used to imply the means or path by which the individual soul unites with God. It is not to be confused with physical exercises alone. Yoga has eight types of disciplines.

The first two, Yama and Niyama, purify the heart and bring about ethical discipline. Yama means abstention from evils of all types—killing,

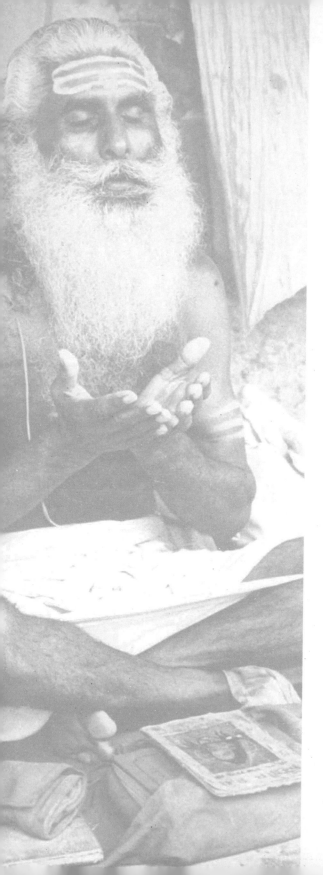

untruth, property, etc. Niyama means observance of purity and practice of austerities.

The next three steps, Asana, Pranayama and Pratyahara are preliminary to Yoga. Asanas are yogic postures which, when practised, steady the mind for concentration and discipline the body. Pranayama are breathing exercises which improve the condition of the lungs, the heart and the nervous system. Pratyahara means shutting out all outward impressions from the mind and looking inward.

The last three steps are called Raja Yoga and include Dharana, Dhyana and Samadhi. Dharana means concentration on any one subject, which could be a light within one's mind. Dhyana or meditation involves an unceasing flow of thoughts and ideas towards this object. Such meditation leads to the final state known as Samadhi, when the subject of the meditation and the object becomes one.

Samadhi itself has two steps. In the first, the conscious samadhi, the yogi attains supernatural powers by the strength of his yogic practices, becomes clairvoyant, adept at mind-reading and thought-transmission. The yogi, who ignores such powers and progresses further, attains the superconscious or nirvikalpa samadhi. The yogi in this stage is a liberated soul.

Samadhi is still practised by some sadhus (holy men), specially in the Himalayas where they live in caves. It is said that they have the ability to slow down their heartbeats. They lie down in a box which is buried ten to twelve feet underground where they remain for many days.

IMPORTANT FAIRS
AND
FESTIVALS OF INDIA

The Indian calendar is one long procession of festivals which are as varied in origin as they are large in number. Some celebrate the birthdays of national heroes and some the eternal cycle of the seasons. Others have origin in religion and in the myths and legends of popular faith. For their proper understanding, therefore, it is essential to form a coherent idea of the religious beliefs of the people.

For a proper appreciation of the festivals connected with the various deities, as far as possible, the major festivals have been mentioned at the end of the description devoted to that particular deity. For this, refer to the section on gods and goddesses.

A Hindu festival is generally characterised by fasting, ablutions, prayer, worship, austerities, vigils, vows, offerings to the gods and holy persons and such other acts of piety and devotion. A Hindu festival is more than a 'festival'. It is cathartic in nature, and, as a means of purification, strengthens the spirit within. They are a lesson in finding enjoyment through renunciation and self-denial. Fasting is one such means of purification and one of the most popular means of spiritual development and self discipline.

In the details of the festivals given below, no specific dates are given as to when the festivals are held, but, only the months are mentioned due the difference between the English and the Hindu calendar. The latter is lunar based.

Maha Kumbha Mela (Fair)

This great religious gathering is held four times in twelve years at Allahabad, Nasik, Haridwar and Ujjain, in January. Legend has it that before the universe took shape, the gods and the demons churned the formless waters as a result of which arose Dhanvantari (from the ocean) carrying in his hands a kumbha (pot) containing nectar. The gods and demons struggled for the possession of the precious liquid. During this struggle, drops of the nectar fell at twelve places in the world. Four of these, Prayag (Allahabad), Nasik, Haridwar and Ujjain are in India and this fair (mela) is held at each of these places in a twelve year cycle. The Allahabad fair is the most famous and one gets an opportunity to see thousands of yogis, sadhus and holy men who descend from their Himalayan abode once in twelve years to attend the fair.

Vasanta Panchami

Mainly a North Indian spring festival, Vasanta Panchami is held in January-February.

The yellow of the flowering mustard fields is the colour of the day. This is reflected in the clothes as well as in the food sprinkled with saffron. In Bengal, the goddess of learning, Saraswati, is worshipped on this day. Field sports and kite flying competitions are part of the celebrations.

Shiva-ratri

See under Shiva, on page 21.

Holi

Celebrated in February-March, there are many legends concerning the origin of this spring festival. The most popular of these legends concerns Prince Prahlad, son of the evil king Hiranyakashipu. Prahlad did not give up worshipping god Vishnu in spite of persecution by his father and his demon aunt Holika. Ultimately when Holika, who was immune to death by fire, took Prahlad in her arms and entered a blazing furnace built for his destruction, it was the wicked Holika who was burnt to ashes by divine intervention, while Prahlad came out unscathed.

Holi is a festival of colours. It marks the end of winter and the advent of spring. Joyous crowds fill the streets, squirting coloured water at one another. In the evening, preceding the colour festival, bonfires are lit symbolising the burning of Holika and the destruction of evil. Holi is also associated with the divine love of Radha and Krishna.

Mahavira Jayanti

Celebrated in March-April, it is the birthday of Vardhamana Mahavira, the twenty-fourth Tirthankara who was born more than 2,500 years ago. For the Jains, it is a day dedicated to his memory. On this day pilgrims from all parts of the country visit the ancient Jain shrines at Girnar and Palitana in Gujarat.

Vaisakhi

Celebrated in April-May, Vaishakhi or Baisakhi is the first day of the month of Vaishakha, the beginning of the Hindu year in some parts of the country. A holy bath in a river or tank is an important feature of the day's observance. For the Sikhs it was on this day that Guru Gobind Singh founded the Khalsa. The river Ganga is believed to have descended to earth on this day.

Buddha Purnima/Jayanti

See under Buddha, on page 40.

Naga Panchami

It is held in July-August. Naga means snake and Panchami is the fifth day of the lunar fortnight. This festival is associated with the great serpent Adisesha or Ananta (infinite) on whom god Vishnu is believed to recline between the dissolution of one universe and the creation of another. Huge cloth effigies of the serpent are made and worshipped. Stone images of snakes are bathed in milk and live cobras are offered milk and flour paste. In West Bengal, instead of the traditional snake deity, the goddess Manasa is worshipped.

Raksha Bandhan

Celebrated in July-August. In the days when the gods warred with the demons, the consort of god Indra tied a rakhi (a silken amulet) on his wrist, by virtue of which, it is said, the god won back his celestial abode from his enemies. On this day sisters tie rakhi on the wrists of their brothers to protect them from evil influences. The person on whose wrist the rakhi is tied is duty bound to offer protection to his sister. There are instances in history when kings or generals, on receiving the rakhi, have led their armies to protect the sender. This is also the day set apart for priests (Brahmins) to change their sacred thread.

Ganesha Chaturthi

See under Ganesha, on page 46.

Janmashtami

See under Krishna, on page 39.

Dussehra

See under Durga, on page 43.

Diwali

See under Lakshmi, on page 56.

Ramanavami

See under Rama, on page 37.

Gurpurb

Celebrated in October-November. For two days and nights preceding the festival, the Guru Granth Sahib is read from the beginning to the end. This is called Akhand Paath. On the day of the festival, the holy book is taken out in a procession through the streets. In December-January the birth anniversary of Guru Gobind Singh, the tenth guru of the Sikhs is celebrated. It was Guru Gobind Singh who welded the Sikhs into a martial community. In 1699, at Anandpur (Punjab), he chose five of the most courageous of the community to form the Khalsa, a militant fraternity of the 'Pure'. They were called the 'Panj Pyara' (the five beloved).

Shraadh

Held in September-October, this is the time to pay homage to one's dead ancestors. The ritual is most effective when performed by a son. The ceremonies performed during this fortnight are a sort of supplement to the funeral ceremonies and are for seeking peace for the soul of the deceased family member. During this period, one neither makes any new purchases nor takes part in any celebration.

SOME IMPORTANT REGIONAL FESTIVALS

Kashmir (Ladakh)

Mela Hemis Gompa (June)—There are a large number of Buddhists in Ladakh and their festivals are associated with ancient monasteries. One of these is held at the famous Hemis Gompa, forty km from Leh. It is the oldest, the biggest and the richest monastery in Ladakh. The fair is held on the tenth day of the fifth Buddhist month every year and lasts for three days. The Lamas dance wearing exotic masks and the low subdued notes of the music being played by them create an air of mystery. The mela (fair) celebrates the birthday of Padma Sambhava, the founder of Lamaism. Masked dancers simulate a combat between good spirits and demons to the sounds of cymbals, drums and pipes.

Punjab/Haryana

Lohri (January)—The festival marks the culmination of winter. Community bonfires are lit and people gather around, singing popular folk songs.

Uttar Pradesh

Car festival at Mathura (March-April)—At the Sri Rangji temple at Brindavan, near Mathura, gorgeous vahanas (chariots) carry the temple deities, Vishnu and his consort Lakshmi, through the streets for ten days. The temple is managed entirely by South Indian Brahmins.

Van Yatra (September-October)—Krishna is believed to have protected the villagers from heavy rains by lifting the Goverdhan mountain. This forest pilgrimage, which commemorates the event, lasts a month and the pilgrims visit all the places connected with the life of Krishna. Goverdhan Puja is held on this day.

Ras Lila—The dance drama depicting episodes from the life of Krishna, is performed by special troupes.

Orissa (Puri)

Jagannath Car Festival (June-July)—King Indradyumna, finding a relic of Krishna, asked Visvakarma, the architect of the gods, to construct a Vishnu temple to house the relic. A beautiful temple was built but Visvakarma abandoned his work due to the undue interference of the king, leaving the image without hands or feet. On the king's plea, Brahma breathed the power of a deity into the idol, which has become one of the most famous ones.

The deity, Jagannath, and his brother and sister are placed in huge chariots forty-five feet high with wheels more than seven feet in diameter. These are pulled by hundreds of devotees to another temple a little distance away, where they are kept for seven days. The event commemorates Krishna's journey to Mathura from Gokul at Kansa's invitation. The chariot procession goes along the broad avenue to Gundicha Mandir, the Lord's summer garden house.

The word 'juggernaut' is said to have originated from the name of this idol.

Rajasthan

Gangaur (March-April)—This spring festival is held in honour of Gauri, the goddess of abundance. Girls pray to the goddess for a good husband. Though the festival is celebrated throughout Rajasthan, the processions in Jaipur and Udaipur have their own charm. In Jaipur, the image is taken out in a procession from the city palace with thousands of people lining the streets to watch it. In Udaipur, a boat procession in the Pichola Lake adds to the gaiety.

Teej (June-July)—This is mainly a women's festival held in honour of Devi (Parvati) who is taken out in a procession with caparisoned

elephants, camels and horses. It is a treat to watch the villagers dressed in bright and colourful clothes on this day. This festival also celebrates the beginning of the monsoon rains.

Pushkar (October-November)—A fair is held by the side of the holy tank at Pushkar, eleven km from Ajmer (130 km from Jaipur). The tank is said to have been created by Brahma himself. Pushkar is also the second place in India having a Brahma temple. The animal fair held here is now internationally famous and thousands of tourists come from all over the world to see it. It is a good opportunity to see the colourful village people from all over Rajasthan.

Andhra Pradesh/Tamil Nadu

Pongal (January)—This three day festival is the biggest event for Tamils. Bhogi-Pongal is the first of the three days followed by Surya-Pongal, dedicated to the Sun. On the third day, Mattu-Pongal, cattle are decorated with flowers and worshipped and fed with pongal (rice cooked in milk and sugar). In many places, money is put in a bundle and tied to the horns of a ferocious bull and unarmed villagers try to seize the bundle. It is a sport requiring great skill.

The Brahmotsavarn (March-April to December-January)—This ten day festival is celebrated with great éclat in the famous temples at Madurai, Kanchipuram and Tirupati. The temple deities are decked in splendid clothes, seated in magnificent carriages and taken out in a procession. Decorated elephants lead the procession and there are fireworks also.

Teppam (February-March)—At Mylapur in the Kapaleeswarar temple and in the Parthasarathy Swamy temple this festival is seen at its best. Seated in a beautifully decorated and illuminated teppam (float), the temple deity is floated and taken round the water-tank to the accompaniment of chanting by the priests.

Madurai River Festival (April-May)—Two deities, Sundaresa and Meenakshi, with pearl crowns on their heads are taken out in a procession. The deities are placed on a golden bull and the procession starts from the Meenakshi temple.

Fire-walking Festival—Held once a year, its time is fixed by the local soothsayer. It is held to ensure a good harvest and to honour the local deities. The chief priest and twelve local youths smear their bodies with turmeric powder and begin a dance that culminates in fire-walking which is done over a long pit filled with live coals. They come out unharmed.

Karnataka

Ugadi (March-April)—This is the New Year's Day and is celebrated with gay abandon.

Dussehra (September-October)—Though Dussehra is celebrated all over India, the elephant procession taken out in Mysore during the festival is very famous. (*See under* the same heading at the beginning of this section)

Head Anointing Ceremony at Sravanabelgola (near Bangalore)— Once every twelve years, the colossal fifty-seven feet high granite statue of Gomateswara (a Jain saint), carved a thousand years ago, is anointed by several thousand Jain monks. They stand on a scaffolding and pour milk, sandalwood paste, gold and silver ornaments and precious stones and many other items on the statue.

Prince Gomateswara gave up his kingdom to become an ascetic and the statue was erected in his honour by his brother.

Kerala

Vishu (March-April)—This is the Malayalee New Year's day. Gifts are exchanged and elders give cash presents to dependents and relatives younger to them.

Onam (August-September)—This is a major harvest festival and also to mark the end of the summer

monsoons. Onam is celebrated in Kerala for four days with a lot of feasting, boat races, dancing and singing. According to legend, Onam is celebrated to welcome the spirit of King Mahabali. At Trichur, elephants take part in a spectacular procession. At Shoranur, Kathakali dancers enact stories of the epic heroes.

The Vallurnkali (boat race) is one of the main attractions of the festival and is best seen at Kottayam and Aranmulai where about a hundred oarsmen row huge graceful boats (odee). In the evening, girls perform the famous clapping dance (Kyekottikali).

ANCIENT SCIENCES
AND
ARTS

THE SCIENCES

Most of the information on the different sciences in ancient India comes from the Vedas, the ancient Hindu books, and also books on specific sciences written during the pre-Vedic and the post-Vedic periods. In the Vedas there are exhaustive references to these sciences and thus we can date them to that period or even earlier.

It is difficult to assign any age to the antiquity of the Vedas. Prof. S Jacobi has found in one of the Rig-Vedic hymns (X. 85. 13) a clear reference to the position of the solstitial colure in 'Uttara Phalguni' (b. Leonis) and Uttara Bhadrapad (a. Andromedae), the year beginning with the summer solstice in the rainy season (Rig Veda, VII. 103. 9) and thereby determined the age of the Rig Veda somewhere between 4500 and 2500 B.C.

In this section only some of the sciences are covered and that too very briefly as the aim of this book is to give a very brief idea of the ancient Hindu sciences and the scientists. To do any justice to the work of the ancient scientists would require voluminous tomes.

Apart from the sciences described here, considerable advances were also made in veterinary science which was known as 'shalihotra'. Many monographs were written on the diseases of horses, elephants and some other animals of common usage at that time. The ancient sastras (books) also contained a detailed sanitary code.

MEDICAL SCIENCE

The science of medicine in the ancient times was carried to a very high degree of perfection by the Hindus. According to Sir William Hunter, "Indian medicine dealt with the whole area of the science. It described the structure of the body, its organs, ligaments, muscles, vessels and tissues. The Materia Medica of the Hindus embraces a vast collection of drugs belonging to the mineral, vegetable and animal kingdoms. Their pharmacy contained ingenious processes of preparation with elaborate directions for the administration and classification of medicines."

Ayurveda

Ayurveda is one of the Upa Vedas (subsidiary Vedas), and in the Mahabharata it is described as the Fifth Veda. Literally, the term ayurveda means the science of life. Prescriptions for the different parts of the day are called 'dinacharya', for the different parts of the night 'ratri charya' and for the different seasons are called 'ritu charya.'

Based on herbs and roots, ayurveda is one of the oldest systems of medicine (3000 B.C.), and is said to have been revealed by Dhanvantari to his pupil Susruta. The history of medicinal plants goes back to the Rig Veda, perhaps the oldest repository of human knowledge. Charaka (300 B.C.) and Susruta, two famous scientists, wrote treatises which are named after them, and are now the two most important works on Indian medicine.

India has 20,000 botanical species, and from time immemorial the Himalayas are rightly considered the greatest treasure house of all kinds of plants and trees. In fact, the world's first ever medicinal plants symposium was held on the slopes of the Himalayas in 700 B.C., and was presided over by the sage Bharadwaja. Experts came from all over to discuss the science of longevity and lectures were delivered by 'vaidyas' (Ayurvedic physicians) on experiments they had carried out with the various herbs to cure chronic diseases.

Ayurveda is still considered very useful and the Indian government has financed and opened ayurvedic colleges all over India. It is considered safer to use ayurvedic drugs as, being natural based, they do not have any side effects. Its popularity in present day society can be gauged from the fact that the ayurvedic centres are opening up all over the world. Very recently, the Soviet Research Centre for Preventive Medicine has opened one in Moscow. Many Indian ayurvedic companies are exporting medicines in large quantities to the West.

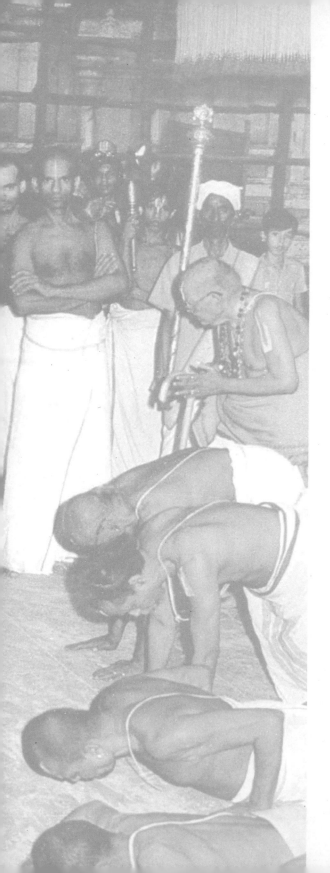

Surgery (Shalya Kriya)

"Their (Hindu) surgery", says Elphinstone, "is as remarkable as their medicine". The sage Susruta is considered the father of surgery. In the ancient times there were more than 127 different types of surgical instruments in common usage and some of them were sharp enough to divide a hair. They included scalpels, lancets, bone-nippers, scoops, forceps, etc.

There were fourteen different types of bandages. The favourite form of splint was made of thin strips of bamboo bound together with string and cut to the length required. This splint was adopted by the British army under the name of the 'patent rattan-cane splint.'

The ancient surgeons conducted amputations and stopped the bleeding by applying pressure and using a cup shaped bandage and boiling oil. They practised lithotomy; performed operations in the abdomen and the uterus; cured hernia, fistula and piles; set broken bones and dislocations; and were experts in the extraction of foreign substances from the body.

Surgery for cataract of the eye and major brain operations were done regularly. A special branch of surgery was devoted to rhinoplasty, or operation for improving a deformed nose and ear and forming new ones. They cured neuralgia and were experts in midwifery and in diseases of women and children.

Surgery was conducted under the following heads:

- Chhedya (excision)
- Lekhya (scarification)
- Vedhya (puncturing)
- Esya (exploration)
- Aharya (extraction)
- Visraya (evacuation)
- Sivya (suturing)

Students practised on tissues and cells of vegetables and upon dead animals. Dissection of dead bodies was also done. Also, a classification of over three hundred bones in the human body had been done at that time.

Atreya and His Academy of Medicine

The sage Atreya may be regarded as the first great teacher of systematic medicine. The composition of the body was divided into three elements— Vayu, Kapha and Pitta. Vayu regulates all the psychic and nervous activities, both sensory and motor. Pitta is responsible for all digestive and metabolic activities including enzyme activities of the body. Kapha serves as a lubricant to all the organs of the body. Blood (rakta) is considered as a vehicle for the three elements (tridhatu) in the human body to keep the internal balance, what is known as the homeostatic to the modern physician. Each of the three elements is subdivided into five different sub-elements.

In a healthy body these elements remain in a state of equilibrium. With improper food this proportion tends to change, leading to diseases. Such disturbances are also caused by psychic factors and seasonal changes. Therefore the physician has to consider the whole body and not just the affected part or organ. His treatment aims at correcting the origin of the disease and not merely provide symptomatic relief.

Atreya had also divided substances into sixty-three types of tastes which were further subdivided into after-taste and comparative and superlative degrees of taste. An understanding of these was necessary for the physician.

MATHEMATICAL SCIENCES

The most extensive cultivation which astronomy received at the hands of the Hindus is in itself a proof of their high proficiency in mathematics. The high antiquity of Hindu astronomy is an argument in support of still greater antiquity of their mathematics. The Hindus were the inventors of the numerals and the great German critic Schlegel says that "the decimal cyphers, the honour of which, next to letters is the most important of human discoveries, has, with the common consent of historical authorities, been ascribed to the Hindus." (Schlegel's *History of Literature*, p 123.)

Sir M. Monier William says "From them (Hindus), the Arabs received not only their first conceptions of algebraic analysis, but also those numerical symbols and decimal notations now current everywhere." (*Indian Wisdom*, p. 124.)

Says W.W. Hunter: "To them (Hindus) we owe the invention of the numeral symbols on the decimal scale, the Indian figures I to 9 being abbreviated forms of initial letters of the numerals themselves, and the zero or 0 representing the first letter of the Sanskrit word for empty, 'Shunya'. The Arabs borrowed them from the Hindus and transmitted them to Europe." (*Imperial Gazetteer*, p. 219, India.)

Algebra

In Algebra, the ancient Hindus understood well the surd roots and the general resolution of equations of the second degree. Algebra developed with astronomy; so one can assume that it was in practice around 3000-2500 B.C.

Sage Bhaskaracharya wrote the book the *Siddhanta Siromani*, containing treatises on algebra and arithmetic. His division of a circle is remarkable for its minute analysis, which is as follows:

60 Vikalpa (seconds)	-	A Kala (minute)
60 Kala	-	A Bhaga (degree)
30 Bhaga	-	A Rasi (sign)
12 Rasi	-	A Bhagana (revolution)

Aryabhata and Bhaskaracharya were well known scientists of the time. Bhaskaracharya, according to Mr Lethbridge, ". . . discovered a mathematical process very nearly resembling the differential calculus of modern European mathematicians."

Geometry

The ancient Hindus made remarkable progress in geometry, which was known in India long before the writing of *Surya Siddhanta* (2000 B.C.), which contains a rational system of trigonometry. It is founded on a geometrical theorem employing the sine of arcs and involves theorems not discovered in Europe till a couple of centuries later.

"They (Hindus) demonstrated various properties of triangles, specially one which expresses the area in terms of the three sides and the knowledge of the proportions of the radius to the circumference of a circle, by applying one measure and one unit to the radius and circumference. This proportion was not known out of India until modern times." (Elphinstone's *History of India*, pp. 129-130).

Researches have brought to light astronomical tables in India which must have been constructed by the principles of geometry and are said to be older than 3000 B.C. (Prof. Wallace in *Edinburgh Encyclopedia*, Geometry, p. 191). Some well known ancient scientists were Aryabhata (A.D. fifth century), Sridharacharya, author of *Patiganita* (A.D. ninth century), Bhaskara (A.D. 629) and Bhaskara II (A.D. 14).

OTHER SCIENCES

Astronomy

Count Bjornstjerna proves conclusively that Hindi astronomy was far advanced even at the beginning of the Kaliyug or iron age of the Hindus, about five thousand years ago (*Theogony of the Hindus*, p. 37).

They knew about the precession of the equinoxes and about the diurnal revolution of the earth on its axis which the priests (Brahmins) discussed in the fifth century B.C. (Colebrooke, *History of India*, p. 132).

The above quotations give some idea of the antiquity of the astronomical science of the ancient Hindus. There are numerous treatises written by famous scientists on astronomy and also astrology which was considered equally important. Some of the well known scientists were Parashar (twelfth century B.C.), Aryabhata and Varahamihira.

"The Hindu astronomers knew about and practised the division of the ecliptic into lunar mansions, the precession of the equinox, the earth's self support in space, the revolution of the moon on her axis, her distance from the earth, the dimensions of the orbits of the planet and the calculation of the eclipses." (Prof. Wilson in Mill's *History of India*, Vol. II, p. 106.)

The ancients knew about the roundness of the earth. In *Aryabhateeya* we read: 'The earth, situated in the middle of the heaven and composed of five elements, is spherical in shape.'

The theory of gravity is thus described in the *Siddhanta Siromani*: 'The earth, owing to its force of gravity, draws all things towards itself, and so they seem to fall towards the earth.'

Another ancient scientist, Gargya, was the first enumerator of constellations and divided the zodiacal belt into twenty-seven equal parts. Varahamihira, son of Gautama, is said to be the first person to identify Jupiter (**Brihaspati**), reference to which is to be found in the Rig Veda.

Towards our time, A.D. 1727, we have Maharaja Jai Singh II, the builder of Jaipur, one of the earliest planned cities and of the famous observatories in Jaipur, Delhi, Varanasi, Mathura and Ujjain. A number of the instruments in these observatories are still working accurately. The sun-dial in Jaipur still gives the time with an accuracy of two seconds! Sawai Jai Singh corrected the Indian almanac also.

Physics and Chemistry

Ancient Indian ideas of physics were closely linked with religion and theology. The universe was classified as being composed of five elements—earth, fire, water, air and ether. There was a belief that elements other than ether were atomic. Indian atomism was certainly independent of Greek influence, for an atomic theory was taught by Pakudha Katyayana, an older contemporary of the Buddha, and was therefore earlier than that of Democritus.

The atom was generally thought to be eternal, but some Buddhists conceived it as occupying space for the minutest possible duration of time, being replaced immediately by another one. Another ancient Indian school maintained that atoms combined into molecules to form objects. Indian atomic theories were not of course based on experiments, but on intuition and logic.

Indian **metallurgists** gained great proficiency in the extraction of metal from ore and in metal casting. **Chemistry** in ancient India was the handmaid, not of technology, but of medicine. Indian chemists did succeed in producing many important alkalies, acids and metallic salts by the simple process of calcination and distillation.

Architecture

Ancient Indians were the earliest to design cities and towns. The ancient book, the *Arthashastra*, contains details on the planning of cities, how to lay out a garden, sink wells, construct tanks, houses, forts, palaces etc. The hydraulic engineers (jala sutradharas) had mastered the art of erecting dams, making bridges and harnessing rivers. Indian architecture

129

influenced the architecture of countries like Borneo, Java, Sumatra, Burma, Malaya, Cambodia etc. Muslim invaders to India, inadvertently, absorbed some of the Indian architectural styles like the dome from the temple mandapam, the pointed arch of the prayer carpet and the mihrab from the arch of the Hindu shrine.

Science of Warfare

War, as an art as well as a science, was well understood in ancient India. The ancient Hindus were adept at naval warfare, as, being a great commercial nation in the ancient world, they were compelled to look to the navy to guard the sea trade routes.

Dhanur Veda, the standard work on Hindu military science being lost, the dissertations on the science found in the Mahabharata, the Agni-Purana and other works are the only sources of information on the subject left to us.

The ancient Hindu tactics of war were very scientific and advanced. The army was divided into seven sections:

1. Uras-centre (breast)
2. Kaksha-flanks
3. Paksha-wings
4. Pratigraha-reserves
5. Koti-vanguard
6. Madhya-centre
7. Prishtha-back.

In the land army, the Hindus also had, besides infantry and cavalry, elephants and chariots. Training of elephants and their use in war was a separate science by itself. There were ancient palm-leaf manuscripts written on the subject.

How to Control and 'Drive' an Elephant

The ancient Hindus had knowledge of more than ninety nerve points in the body of the elephant, and by pressing on them by the toes or with a specially shaped iron rod (ankush), the driver of the elephant could make it obey his commands, such as 'turn around', 'attack the enemy', 'turn right' or 'turn left', etc.

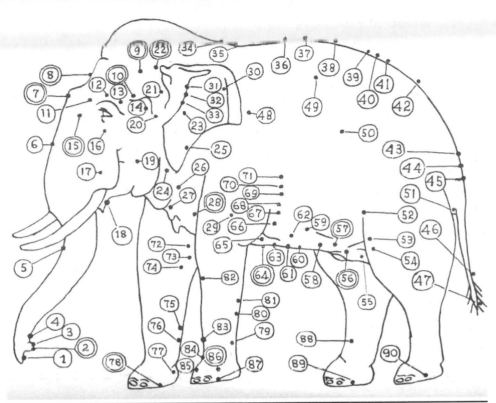

Nerve centre as numbered in diagram above.	Reflex action caused by pressure on nerves of the elephant
1.	Will twist trunk.
2.	Will straighten trunk.
3, 4, 5, 39, 40, 41, 42.	Will get frightened; excited.
6, 11, 12, 14, 18, 21, 30, 35.	Will come under control; lose its sense of feeling.
7, 8, 9, 10, 15, 22, 28, 51, 56, 57, 64, 78, 86, 87, 88, 89, 90.	Can die if pressure is hard.
13, 25, 60, 61, 63.	Will get infuriated.
16, 58, 69, 70, 71.	Will kneel down, go down on elbows.
17.	Will move backwards.
19.	Will push with its shoulders.
20, 24, 26, 36, 37, 46, 48, 29, 45, 65, 66, 67, 68.	Will stop.
23, 27, 34, 38, 49.	Will bend its head to offer seat.
31, 32, 33, 43, 44, 45, 47, 72, 73, 74.	Will walk or move forward.
50.	Will stay still; put its trunk on the ground.
52.	Will get up and run.
53, 54, 55, 59, 62.	Will turn around.
75, 76, 77, 83, 84, 85.	Will raise its forefoot for rider to climb onto its head.
79, 80, 81.	Will bring hindfoot forward.
82.	Will bring hindfoot backwards.

According to Prof. Max Dunker, elephants given by Chandragupta to Seleucus 'a few years later decided the day of Ipsus in Phrygia against Antigonus, a victory which secured to Seleucus the territory of Syria, Asia Minor, etc.' Elephant drivers at that time in Greece were called 'Indians'.

Vyuha. The array of forces in battle was a science by itself. These were called 'vyuha', and were named after objects they resembled. For example, Makara-vyuha meànt the army drawn up in the shape of Makara, a sea monster, or Suchi-mukha or needle point array.

The array or the vyuha was either for attack or for defence and a good general could turn the tide of battle by pre-empting the enemy vyuha and directing his army to form a counter one. It was like a deadly chess game. Each of the vyuhas had subdivisions numbering five to seventeen. In the Mahabharata, during the epic battle, Yudhishthira suggests to Arjuna, in the heat of the battle, to adopt the Suchi-mukha or Needle-point array while the former is thinking of Vajra (thunderbolt) array.

Ancient Hindu weapons were divided into five sections:

1. Yantra-mukta: missiles thrown with an instrument.

2. Hasta-mukta: those thrown by hand.

3. Muktamukta: weapons which may or may not be thrown, like spears, javelins, etc.

4. Weapons which are not thrown, like mace, swords etc.

5. Natural weapons like fists, kicking with the feet, etc.

Each section had subdivisions and there were special techniques for using each weapon. There were masters proficient in these techniques and sometimes a warrior would spend ten years or more for acquiring the knowledge from these masters or gurus.

Archery was cultivated most assiduously by the ancient Hindus, specially on horseback and they could shoot four to nine arrows at a time. They also used fire arrows and boomerang-like arrows.

Military espionage was highly developed and the *Arthashastra* written by Kautilya describes the various types of spies, their training and usefulness to the kings and the army.

THE ARTS

MUSIC

According to Col. Tod, "All account of the state of musical science amongst the Hindus of early ages appears to have attained a theoretical precision yet unknown to Europe." According to Anne C. Wilson, "...their (the Hindus') system of music, as a written science, is the oldest in the world. Its principal features were given long ago in Vedic writings." India's devotion to music goes back to pre-historic times and there are references in the religious texts and other ancient treatises which suggest that music had achieved a very high degree of sophistication as far back as three thousand years ago. From the beginning of the Christian era, a wealth of literature on the science and art of music has sprung up.

The 'Gandharva Veda', the masterpiece on this 'science and art' is unfortunately lost and references to it in the Sanskrit works alone remain to point to the high principle on which the Hindu science of music was based. One of the most ancient authorities on music, dance and drama is Bharat, author of *Natya Shastra* written about A.D. third century, the most celebrated work of its kind in the country's tradition. Bharat mentions other authorities on music with whose opinion he disagrees, which shows that the study of music was prevalent in the country much before his time.

In the traditional culture of India, music envelops the entire life of man in a shell of melodic sound. The folk tradition has been a great source, and there are references to the 'songs of hamlets' and 'songs of the forests' even in ancient Vedic literature. This music was rich in spontaneity and lyricism. The religious music that developed out of the singing of the Vedic hymns gave it a conscious grammar and control of the lines of evolutionary growth. The evolution of the Indian musical

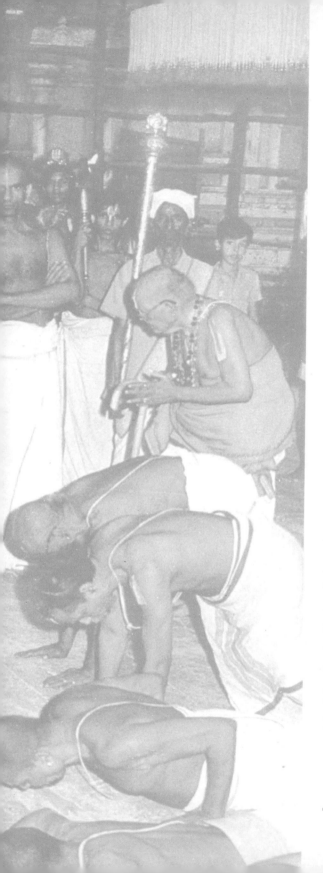

scale spanned many centuries. The recited metrical hymns of the Rig Veda sprouted wings to become the chants of the Sama Veda. The notes used for building up the melody increased from three to five and then to seven. Flats or sharps of five, of the seven main notes, raised the spectrum to twelve fairly easily distinguishable notes. But the whole span was also more minutely divided into twenty-two micro-tonal steps of less than a semi-tone. This means that even a specific flat or sharp note can be found in actual singing in delicately shaded, aesthetically flavoured variations. These demand a fine ear and repeated hearing. The scales were later grouped under certain gradations of musical sound which evolved into a scale of seven notes or 'swaras'. This scale, incidentally, also forms the basis of Western music.

The concept of melody, as embodied in what is known as **raga**, is one of the many unique features of Indian music. Melodic development is conceived as an unbroken process and is evolved by means of fine middle tones lying between the notes of the scale. The notes serve only as landmarks.

A raga is neither a scale nor a mode. It is a distinct melodic pattern representing a combination of five, six or seven notes chosen from the musical scale. The prominence of certain fixed notes and the sequence of conjugate notes go to differentiate one raga from another. Tonal embellishments known as 'gamaks' and rhythmic forms of intonations also vary with the ragas and thereby determine the individuality of each. These ragas form quite a large variety. Each raga is associated with the specific hour of the day or night, or sometimes with a particular season, and is designed, by virtue of its constitution, to express a certain mood or sentiment. This time theory, which governs the raga, is the most unique feature of the music of North India. **Tala** is yet another special feature of Indian music, being an organised combination of beats on which rhythmic structure is based. Some important ragas are listed below:

Bilawal is a moving raga, depicting a sprightly, joyous mood.

Lalit is one of the most popular morning melodies designed to unfold a serene mood.

Todi is also a morning raga, delineating a profound mood with a touch of pathos.

Sarang is known for its benign grandeur and is conventionally rendered at mid-day.

Bhoop, an evening raga, is noted for its soft caressive charm.

Des, rendered during the second quarter of the night, is designed to convey an intense mood of love.

Malkauns, a midnight raga, sombre yet sensitive in its contents, is immensely popular.

Bhairavi. The effect of this raga is to inspire the mind with the feeling of approaching dawn and dew-dropping freshness of early morning. Convention has it that it can be rendered and heard as a concluding piece in a recital at any hour of the day or night. The raga affords ample scope to portray any feeling or mood.

Megh Malhar is descriptive of the effects of an approaching thunderstorm and rain.

Deepak. This raga is now extinct. It is said that no one could sing it and live. Its effect is to light the lamps and cause the body of the singer to produce flames by which he dies.

There are about three hundred ragas out of which a hundred or so are common. The ragas are further divided into female forms called **raginis**.

SOME COMMON INDIAN MUSICAL INSTRUMENTS

Shankh (Conch-shell)

The shankh or conch-shell as a musical instrument was used as far back as 2500 B.C. and is still found in use all over India. It was used in war as a heraldic instrument. Though not very sophisticated, it is used in folk music and prayers. It is played at the beginning and at the end of religions ceremonies.

Chimta (Iron Fork)

The chimta seen in various parts of India is a 'jingle johnny' with small platelets. It is an iron fork, a metre long, on the arms of which sets of brass discs are loosely fixed. The instrument is shaken or beaten against the palm rhythmically as an accompaniment to prayers, folk-songs and dances.

Dholak (Drum)

A two-headed drum, the dholak is suspended from the neck, tied to the waist or kept in the lap. A very basic folk instrument, it is common all over India. It is found in hundreds of varieties and the shape and size varies from region to region, from the huge 'dhak'of Bengal to the 'damru' held in one hand and used by Lord Shiva during his dance of destruction, the 'tandava'.

Bansuri (Flute)

Of the two kinds of this wind instrument, the horizontal kind is most popular in India spanning tribal, folk and classical concert music.

Ghungroo (Ankle Bells)

Ankle bells are a must for dancers and are a symbol of their profession. When a dancer makes his or her debut, the tying of the ghungroo is an indispensable ceremony. The ghungroo consists of small round hollow metallic bells with a small round metallic pebble inside to produce a rattle. About thirty or forty of them are fixed to a cloth belt which is tied to the ankles. They are not used in art music as they do not produce a definite pitch or sound.

Harmonium

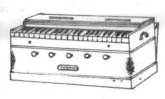

It is developed from reed aerophones like the Chinese 'Sheng'. From India the reed organ went to Europe through Russia and then came back with the traders and took the form of the modern harmonium. It is a box-like structure with bellows, black and white keys and an air chamber and reeds. It became very popular as it does not require any tuning and has a loud sound. It is out of bounds for classical musicians as it does not produce the delicate oscillations of the musical notes.

Pungi/Been

A common folk wind instrument mainly used by snake charmers. The upper part consists of a dried gourd into which wind is blown, which under pressure is released through bamboo valves into two reed/bamboo pipes connected to the lower end of the gourd. One pipe provides the drone while the other is used for playing.

Sarangi

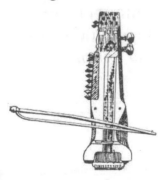

One of the most important of the Indian bow and string instruments, it is at once a typical folk and a concert instrument. The concert model is made of one block of wood sixty centimetres high. The hollow body is wide, but waisted at the bottom and covered with parchment and acts as the main sound box. The principal strings, four in number, are of gut. The most notable aspect is the finger technique which is not used in the case of any other instrument. The side of the finger nails are used for stopping the strings (a technique found as far away as Yugoslavia and Greece). There are hundreds of different folk varieties of this instrument found in North India.

Sarod

It is a concert lute with a body of wood and waisted. The fingerboard has a steel veneer. There are four principal strings, four subsidiary strings, two drones and a dozen sympathetic vibrators. It is said to have descended from a Central Asian instrument called 'ud' meaning short-necked lute.

Shehnai

A twin reed wind instrument, it has a tube for the central body ending in a flare. There are many folk variations and names for this instrument. It is likely to be connected with the 'Zurna' of Central Asia. It is commonly played at classical concerts. One of its finest exponents is Ustad Bismillah Khan.

Sitar

A long-necked lute, it has a spherical gourd at the lower end. The neck has convex brass frets which in some sitars can be moved to the required scale. There are five main metal strings, two drones and eleven to seventeen thin strings which go under the main ones for additional resonance. The bridge (of bone or antler horn) is usually a double one. Before the eighteenth century, the sitar was not considered a respectable instrument but is now one of the most popular concert instruments.

Tabla

A two-piece drum set, of which one is called tabla and the other dagga, but collectively known as tabla. The dagga is made of wood and is long and narrow at the top while the

tabla is smaller, rounder and broader at the top and is made of metal. The membranes are held on with the help of leather thongs which can be tightened with the help of round wooden pieces put between the body and the thongs. The tabla is played with the right hand and the dagga with the left. The dagga normally cannot be tuned.

Tanpura

Looks like a sitar but has only four strings and is basically a drone. The sound box is normally made out of a hollowed-out pumpkin which is dried in a special way over a kitchen fireplace, taking years. The long fingerboard has metallic strings which are plucked one by one to produce a luxuriance of tone to provide a background with other instruments or voice. The South Indian variety replaces the pumpkin with wood.

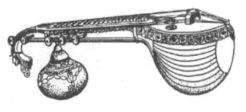

Veena

A stringed instrument as popular as the sitar. There are many varieties of the Veena, the most popular among them being called the Saraswati Veena. Saraswati is the goddess of learning and is normally shown playing this instrument. It has a double gourd (resonators) and the long fingerboard ends in a U shape. The wooden bridge is a complex unit with a curved auxiliary part with drone strings passing on each side. The main bridge has four metal strings for the melody.

CLASSICAL DANCES

The art of dancing in India goes back to the ancient times. Hindu dances are said to originate from Lord Shiva's famous 'tandava' dance. The first rules of Hindu dances were codified by sage Bharata between

A.D. 100-300 in a book called the *Natya Shastra*. Hindu dance is closely linked with emotions. It is a perfect harmony between classical music and bodily movement. In fact, its objective can be summed up to create different moods in the minds of the spectators. Almost all Hindu dances are performed barefoot and are composed of: Abhinaya—facial and bodily expression, Mudras—hand gestures and Gati—footwork. Classical Hindu dances are mainly of four types—Bharatnatyam, Kathak, Kathakali and Manipuri. These are mainly religious in origin. One particular type, Bharatnatyam was performed in temples by girls (Devdasis) but in course of time the dance became secularised, due partly to the demands of the Mughal rulers, and the girls became outcasts.

Bharatnatyam

Originally a temple dance performed by Devdasis (temple dancers), it originated in South India and as is now practised, follows most clearly the *Natya Shastra* and is the most classical in form. It has been preserved through oral or rote tradition. It is a solo dance and its classical poses have been sculpted on the walls of many South Indian temples. It was originally performed by women only. The performance is divided into six sections of varying lengths. The chanter guides the pure dance sections by reciting rhythmic syllables to which the drum beats and the steps of the dancer must correspond exactly. The interpretative sections use a complex technique of hand gestures (mudras) combined with highly stylised facial and dance movements to interpret sung texts from the *Gita-Govinda*, the *Ramayana*, etc.

Kathakali

A pantomimic dance-drama of Kerala (South India), it is mainly performed by male dancers. It depicts incidents from Lord Rama's life with the acting based on the *Natya Shastra*. Thus, it has the vigour of the folk-dance while at the same time retaining a classical grace.

The main sentiment displayed is heroism with emphasis on the terrific. Hence, women play no part in it, their roles being acted by men. Both Bharatnatyam and Kathakali accept the *Natya Shastra* as their authority, but while the former is a dance, usually solo, Kathakali is a dance-drama, a ballet in which several characters appear on the stage at the same time. A Kathakali performance may go on for the whole night.

Kathak

A very popular dance from Punjab and Uttar Pradesh (North India), it is based on mythological stories about Lord Krishna and Radha. Mainly performed by women, the dancers pay great attention to footwork strictly following the rhythmic accompaniment of the tabla (drum), whose reverberations are reproduced by the jingling of bells attached to the anklets. Because of its over-emphasis on technique and absence of emotional expression, some critics assign an inferior position to this dance.

Manipuri

Performed by the hill people of Manipur in North-east India, the dance depicts the Radha-Krishna theme. The dance, performed by men and women is usually done in a circle or semi-circle, in imitation of Krishna's rasa dance. Songs from the *Gita-Govinda* usually accompany the performance. The rasa-lila is really a full scale opera combining elements of dance and chorus. It is a dance of lavish colour with the girls wearing long, wide skirts which are extremely decorative, with mirrors and mica sewn on.

PAINTING

From extant records, literary and archaeological, the art of painting seems to have achieved a high popularity and an equally high aesthetic and technical standard in the ancient times in India. No specimens exist since paintings were generally done on perishable materials such as textiles, leaves, barks of trees, wood, or on semi-permanent materials such as plastered walls. Brahminical and Buddhist literatures dating back to the pre-Christian era contain numerous references to paintings of various types and their techniques. Paintings on pottery and on walls or rock cut caves are some examples of pre-historic and historic paintings but it is only around the fifth century B.C. that we have some record of early paintings. The *Kamasutra* of Vatsyayana (500 B.C.) lists painting as one of the sixty-four 'kalas' or fine arts and mentions paints, brushes and drawing-boards as essential accessories of an average citizen. There is also a reference to six limbs of painting.

The treatise, Brhat Samhita (A.D. sixth century) introduces such technical details as the preparation of the ground for murals, application of colours, methods of shading, mood and movement and classification of paintings. A paste of powdered rock, clay, cow-dung, vegetable fibre and molasses was used as the ground for the frescos. The principal colours used were red ochre, vivid red (kumkum), lamp-black, chalk-white etc. Examples of fine wall paintings are at Kanheri-Aurangabad (A.D. sixth century), Bagh (A.D. 500), Ajanta (A.D. sixth century), Badami (A.D. sixth century) etc. The theme is religious but in their inner meaning and spirit nothing could be more secular, courtly and sophisticated. The Ajanta caves are basically temples cut into the mountains by the artist-priests. The frescos there have a unity of composition, and a clearness and simplicity of line. At Ajanta, religious devotion fused architecture, sculpture and painting into a happy unity and produced one of the sovereign monuments of Hindu art.

Till about the thirteenth-fourteenth century, palm leaves were used for the paintings and they were basically for illustrating manuscripts or miniatures of murals. After the thirteenth century, paper was used more regularly but the form and technique continued uninterrupted from the earlier tradition of Bagh and Ajanta.

During the fourteenth–fifteenth century, the advent of Islam as a political power led to a cultural renaissance. Though the traditional style of painting survived in Western India under the patronage of the middle-class, mostly Jains, this style was further influenced by the revival of the Krishna movement in the fifteenth century. But apart from this Western Indian School of painting, some of the Sultans and Hindu potentates were patrons of art and culture and different regional court styles flourished during their respective reigns.

The Sultanate (Muslim) painting shows an attempt to arrive at a fusion of the newly introduced Persian and Indian traditional styles. Out of this emerged three major sub-styles, the Mughal, Rajasthani and Deccani Schools (A.D. sixteenth century). The Mughal style received a fillip under Emperor Akbar and developed further under Jahangir when nature was the main theme. During Shah Jahan's time, Mughal painting achieved technical perfection but the theme was stereo-typed and confined to the four walls, the durbar. Aurangzeb was against art and the downfall of Mughal painting started during his reign. Around the same time, the regional sub-schools of the Rajasthani group flourished in centres like Mewar, Amber, Bundi, Jodhpur etc. A vigorous art style also flourished in the hills of Basohli, Mandi, Kangra, Guler, Bilaspur etc.

Through it all we have to understand that Indian painting seeks to represent not things but feelings, not to represent but to suggest.

SCULPTURE

The art of sculpture was practised by Indians from ancient times but the materials used were impermanent like clay and wood, hence we do not have many examples from those early times, except for some clay and terracotta figurines of the early Indus Valley Civilisation (3000 B.C.). These testify to the skill of Indian sculptors. The oldest surviving stone figures go back to the Ashok period (sixth century B.C.) and they show a skill so highly developed that it proves that the art had behind it many centuries in growth. Some extant sculptures of the Mauryan period points to their religious character. Folk religion, cult

images and objects and their accession set the standards of plastic modelling in ancient and medieval India.

Buddhism set up definite obstacles to both painting and sculpture but gradually this puritanism relaxed and images of Buddha were soon being made. Sculptures relating to the Brahmanical and Jain creeds dating to second and third century B.C. have been discovered at Mathura. The post Mauryan period saw the development of the Bhakti movement which gave a fillip to the sculpture of various divinities, specially folk ones.

During the Gupta dynasty (A.D. 320–530) there was a phenomenal development in art and sculptural representation of the divinities were at their best. During this period, many books were compiled on iconography and rules were codified for the making of various divine figures, their different poses, hand gestures etc. The Gupta sculpture had a new aesthetic quality and the youthful human form became the pivot as opposed to the earlier Kusana School (A.D. 120) which retained the volume and physicality of the earlier folk art to a great extent. The sculptures of the post Gupta period, though relating to some extent to the earlier classical idiom, came to be characterised by regional variations and the skillful sculptors practised their art through the medium of stone, bronze and clay. During this period, some of the medieval images of the principal sectarian deities came to be smothered with heavy decorative details not so obtrusively noticeable in classical art.

The sculpture of the period from A.D. 1206 to 1761 continues the elegance and grace of the early medieval tradition in the massive monumentality of the mid-medieval phase and the 'baroque' splendour of the late medieval centuries.

Eastern India is represented by such magnificent monuments as those at Bhubaneswar, Puri, Konark, Jaipur and Khiching. The culmination of Kalinga art is probably the stone temple at Konark. On the jagmohan of this temple there is not an inch of space which is not covered with sculpture and the variety of themes is tremendous. The Chalukyan temples of the later phase in the South (Karnataka) are characterised by a profusion of decoration almost subduing the main figures, and are the main characteristic of this art.

In Gujarat, during the time of Vastupala, fine temples were built at Mt. Abu (Rajasthan) which are famous for their very fine filigree like marble carvings, specially on the ceilings.

The most remarkable monuments presenting a wealth of iconography, unsurpassed anywhere, is the group of temples built by the Chandelas at Khajuraho around the A.D. tenth–twelfth century. It is not only the conographic wealth, Brahminical and Jain, but also the sculptural survey of the history of the dynasty.

During the fourteenth century, in the Vijayanagara period, a new phase of art arose. Though representing a decadent phase on account of its stylisation, it was still a vital factor. The Vithalla temple at Hampi represents the high watermark of this art. This phase has probably presented the largest number of secular portrait sculptures.

Everywhere in India, in the millennium before the coming of the Muslims, the art of the sculptor, inspired by religion, produced masterpieces. The pretty statue of Vishnu from Sultanpur, the gigantic three-faced Shiva (Trimurti) carved in deep relief in the caves at Elephanta, the graceful dancing Shiva, or Nataraja, cast in bronze by the Chola artisans of Tanjore, the lovely stone deer of Mamallapuram and the handsome Shiva of Perur—these are evidences of the spread of the carver's art into every province of India.

The same motives and methods crossed the frontiers of India proper in the ancient times and produced masterpieces from Turkestan and Cambodia to Java and Ceylon.

Hindu Gods and Goddesses

PURANIC DEITIES (THE TRINITY)

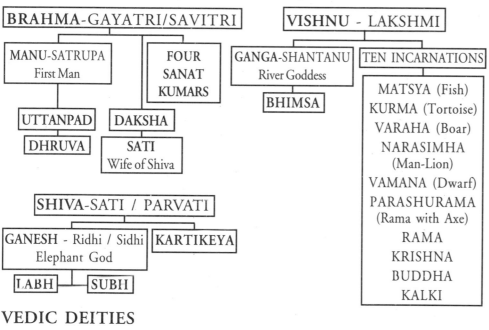

BRAHMA-GAYATRI/SAVITRI

- **MANU-SATRUPA** — First Man
  - **UTTANPAD**
    - **DHRUVA**
- **FOUR SANAT KUMARS**
  - **DAKSHA**
    - **SATI** — Wife of Shiva

VISHNU - LAKSHMI

- **GANGA-SHANTANU** — River Goddess
  - **BHIMSA**
- **TEN INCARNATIONS**
  - MATSYA (Fish)
  - KURMA (Tortoise)
  - VARAHA (Boar)
  - NARASIMHA (Man-Lion)
  - VAMANA (Dwarf)
  - PARASHURAMA (Rama with Axe)
  - RAMA
  - KRISHNA
  - BUDDHA
  - KALKI

SHIVA-SATI / PARVATI

- **GANESH** - Ridhi / Sidhi — Elephant God
  - **LABH** — **SUBH**
- **KARTIKEYA**

VEDIC DEITIES

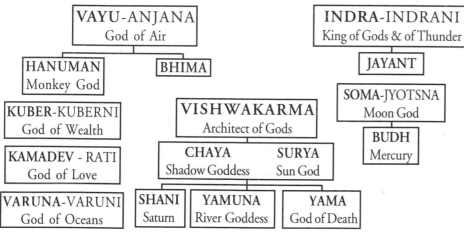

VAYU-ANJANA — God of Air

- **HANUMAN** — Monkey God
- **BHIMA**

KUBER-KUBERNI — God of Wealth

KAMADEV - RATI — God of Love

VARUNA-VARUNI — God of Oceans

VISHWAKARMA — Architect of Gods

- **CHAYA** — Shadow Goddess
- **SURYA** — Sun God
  - **SHANI** — Saturn
  - **YAMUNA** — River Goddess
  - **YAMA** — God of Death

INDRA-INDRANI — King of Gods & of Thunder

- **JAYANT**

SOMA-JYOTSNA — Moon God

- **BUDH** — Mercury

Note:
- Deities usually do not have children but take incarnations (to fight the evil forces).
- Only important deities are featured in these charts.
- Vedic Deities are older but lost their importance to later Puranic Deities.
- The lighter names in the boxes represent the consorts/wives.

MOTHER GODDESS—(Shakti)

Terrible Form	Benign Form
Kali*	Bhuvaneshwari*
Tara*	Kamala*
Chinnamasta*	Sodasi*
Bagala*	Shailputri‡
Dhumavati*	Skandamata‡
Bhairavi*	Parvati
Matangi*	Mahagauri‡
Chandraghanta‡	Siddhidhatri‡
Kushmanda‡	Indrani‡
Kalratri‡	Vaishnavi†
Katyayani‡	Kaumari†
Chamunda†	Lakshmi
Varahi†	Saraswati
Brahmani†	
Maheshwari†	

* Ten Mahavidyas (Manifestations)
† Seven Matrikas (Mothers)
‡ Nine Durgas (Nav-Durgas)

Some Sacred Cities of India

METRO CITIES

SACRED CITIES

Some Sacred Rivers and Mountains of India

KAILASH

DELHI

GOVERDHAN

KAMAGIRI

Yamuna

Ganga

Gandak

Sabarmati

INDIA

KOLKATA

MALAYAGIRI

Godavari

MUMBAI

CHENNAI

SACRED RIVERS
METRO CITIES
SACRED MOUNTAINS

GLOSSARY

Aarti	Form of worship in which a tray of lighted oil lamps is waved in a circular pattern before the deity
Achal	Immovable
Agni	Fire
Ahimsa	Non-violence
Amrita	Nectar of immortality
Ankush	Elephant goad
Apsara	Nymph, celestial dancers at the court of Indra
Ardha-narishwara	Half-man, half-woman, one of the forms of Shiva
Ashrama	Hermitage
Asura	Demon
Atman	True self, the eternal soul
Avatara	Manifestation, incarnation
Bana-linga	Stone from the riverbed used as a linga
Bhagvada-Gita	Sacred book of the Hindus
Bhakti	Devotion/folk movement
Bindu	Point, dot
Brahmachari	Bachelor, celibate
Brahmin	Priest/Supreme Reality
Chakra	Wheel
Chal	Movable
Chandra	Moon
Damru	Small drum
Dev, Deva, Devta	Male deity
Devdasi	Temple dancer
Devi	Female deity
Dharma	Religion/Righteousness

Gada	Club, mace
Ganga	Sacred river
Garuda	Divine bird (half man)/Vehicle of Lord Vishnu
Gayatri mantra	Most important of the Vedic mantras specially for invoking the Sun god
Gopika	Cowherd woman
Guru	Teacher, spiritual guide
Gurukul	School
Gyan	Knowledge
Hanuman	Monkey god
Jal	Water
Jamuna	Sacred river
Jayanti	Birthday
Jhanki	Tableaux
Kalpa	A day of Brahma
Kama	Lust
Kantha	Throat
Krodha	Anger
Kshatriya	Warrior community
Kusha grass	A type of sacred grass
Lakshmi	Goddess of wealth
Linga, Lingam	Phallic symbol/Representation of Shiva
Lobha	Greed
Mahabharata	Sanskrit epic describing the great war between the Pandavas and the Kauravas
Mala	Garland, rosary
Mantra	Sacred saying, divine power transmitted as word
Mata, Matrika	Mother
Mela	Fair
Moksha	Liberation from the cycle of birth and rebirths
Mudra	Hand gesture, pose
Naga	Snake
Naraka	Hell

Neel	Blue
Nirguna	Without form, formless worship
Nirvana	Union with the Supreme
Padma	Lotus flower
Pati	Lord, master, husband
Prasad	Food left over after being offered to the deity
Puja	Prayers, worship
Purana	A narrative work dealing with the ancient kings, sages and gods
Pushpak	Flying chariot of Lord Kubera
Raga	Melody pattern in Indian classical music
Rakta	Blood
Ramayana	Sanskrit epic describing Lord Rama's search for Sita, who is abducted by Ravana
Ratri	Night
Rishi	Sage
Saguna	Having a form/A type of worship
Salagrama	Ammonite stone considered sacred
Sanyas	To renounce
Shakti	Prowess/Female energy, divinity
Shani	Saturn
Shankh	Conch-shell
Shastras	Books
Sisya, Shisya	Pupil
Shraadh	Ceremony performed periodically in honour of one's ancestors
Surya	Sun
Swaraga	Heaven
Swastika	Tantric symbol
Tandava	Dance of destruction by Lord Shiva
Tantra (ism)	Form of Yogic practice
Tilak	Mark put on the forehead
Upanishad	Vedic scripture

Vahana	Vehicle
Vaidya	Vedic physician
Varuna	God of the oceans
Vedas	Ancient Hindu scriptures (1700–1200 B.C.)
Vidya	Knowledge, education
Yagna, Yagya	Sacrificial fire, religious ceremony
Yaksha	Tree spirit
Yama	God of death
Yantra	A diagram/Visual form of Mantra
Yoga	A technique of physical and spiritual training